Learning RabbitMQ

Build and optimize efficient messaging applications
with ease

Martin Toshev

BIRMINGHAM - MUMBAI

Learning RabbitMQ

First published: December 2015

Production reference: 1171215

Published by Packt Publishing Ltd.
Livery Place
35 Livery Street
Birmingham B3 2PB, UK.

ISBN 978-1-78398-456-5

www.packtpub.com

Credits

Author
Martin Toshev

Reviewers
Van Thoai Nguyen
Héctor Veiga

Commissioning Editor
Ashwin Nair

Acquisition Editor
Vinay Argekar

Content Development Editor
Kirti Patil

Technical Editor
Danish Shaikh

Copy Editor
Vibha Shukla

Project Coordinator
Nidhi Joshi

Proofreader
Safis Editing

Indexer
Hemangini Bari

Graphics
Disha Haria

Production Coordinator
Arvindkumar Gupta

Cover Work
Arvindkumar Gupta

About the Author

Martin Toshev is a software developer and Java enthusiast with more than eight years of experience and vast expertise originating from projects in areas such as enterprise Java, social networking, source code analysis, Internet of Things, and investment banking in companies such as Cisco and Deutsche Telekom. He is a graduate of computer science from the University of Sofia. He is also a certified Java professional (SCJP6) and a certified IBM cloud computing solution advisor. His areas of interest include a wide range of Java-related technologies (Servlets, JSP, JAXB, JAXP, JMS, JMX, JAX-RS, JAX-WS, Hibernate, Spring Framework, Liferay Portal, and Eclipse RCP), cloud computing technologies, cloud-based software architectures, enterprise application integration, and relational and NoSQL databases. Martin is one of the leaders of the Bulgarian Java Users group (BGJUG), a regular speaker at Java conferences, and one of the organizers behind the jPrime conference in Bulgaria (http://jprime.io/).

About the Reviewers

Van Thoai Nguyen has worked in the software industry for a decade in various domains. In 2012, he joined BuzzNumbers as one of the core senior software engineers, where he had opportunities to design, implement, and apply many cool technologies, tools, and frameworks. A RabbitMQ cluster was employed as the backbone of the real-time data processing platform, which includes various data collectors, data filtering, enrichment, and storage using a sharded cluster of MongoDB and SOLR. He is still maintaining the open source .NET RabbitMQ client library, Burrow.NET (`https://github.com/vanthoainguyen/Burrow.NET`), which he built during the time he worked for BuzzNumbers. This library is still being used in many different applications in that company. Van is interested in clean code and design, SOLID principle, and BIG data. You can read his blog at `http://thoai-nguyen.blogspot.com.au/`.

Héctor Veiga is a software engineer specializing in real-time data integration and processing. Recently, he has focused his work on different cloud technologies, such as AWS, to develop scalable, resilient, and high-performing applications with the latest open source technologies, such as Scala, Akka, or Apache Spark. Additionally, he has a strong foundation in messaging systems, such as RabbitMQ and AMQP. He also has a master's degree in telecommunications engineering from the Universidad Politécnica de Madrid and a master's degree in information technology and management from the Illinois Institute of Technology.

He currently works as part of the Connected Driving real-time data collection team and is actively developing scalable applications to ingest and process data from several different sources. He utilizes RabbitMQ heavily to address their messaging requirements. In the past, he worked at Xaptum Technologies, a company dedicated to M2M technologies.

Héctor also helped with the reviewing process of *RabbitMQ Cookbook* and *RabbitMQ Essentials*, both from *Packt Publishing*.

www.PacktPub.com

Support files, eBooks, discount offers, and more

For support files and downloads related to your book, please visit www.PacktPub.com.

Did you know that Packt offers eBook versions of every book published, with PDF and ePub files available? You can upgrade to the eBook version at www.PacktPub.com and as a print book customer, you are entitled to a discount on the eBook copy. Get in touch with us at service@packtpub.com for more details.

At www.PacktPub.com, you can also read a collection of free technical articles, sign up for a range of free newsletters and receive exclusive discounts and offers on Packt books and eBooks.

https://www2.packtpub.com/books/subscription/packtlib

Do you need instant solutions to your IT questions? PacktLib is Packt's online digital book library. Here, you can search, access, and readPackt's entire library of books.

Why subscribe?

- Fully searchable across every book published by Packt
- Copy and paste, print, and bookmark content
- On demand and accessible via a web browser

Free access for Packt account holders

If you have an account with Packt at www.PacktPub.com, you can use this to access PacktLib today and view 9 entirely free books. Simply use your login credentials for immediate access.

I would like to thank all of the people that supported me during the process of writing this book and especially my mother Milena, my beloved Tsveti and my grandmother Maria. Without them this would not have been possible.

Table of Contents

Preface

Learning RabbitMQ provides you with a practical guide for the notorious message broker and covers the essentials required to start using it. The reader is able to build up knowledge along the way—starting from the very basics (such as what is RabbitMQ and what features does it provide) and reaching the point where more advanced topics, such as RabbitMQ troubleshooting and internals, are discussed. Best practices and important tips are provided in a variety of scenarios; some of them are related to external systems that provide integration with the message broker or that are integrated as part of the message broker in the form of a RabbitMQ plugin. Practical examples are also provided for most of these scenarios that can be applied in a broader context and used as a good starting point.

An example system called **CSN (Corporate Social Network)** is used to illustrate the various concepts provided throughout the chapters.

Each chapter ends with an Exercises section that allows the reader to test his understanding on the presented topic.

What this book covers

Chapter 1, Introducing RabbitMQ, provides you with a brief recap on enterprise messaging and a short overview of RabbitMQ along with its features. Other similar technologies are mentioned and an installation guide for the message broker is provided at the end of the chapter. The basic terminology behind RabbitMQ such as exchanges, queues, and bindings is introduced.

Chapter 2, Design Patterns with RabbitMQ, discusses what messaging patterns can be implemented using RabbitMQ, including point-to-point, publish-subscribe, request-reply, and message router types of communication. The patterns are implemented using the building blocks provided by the message broker and using the Java client API.

Chapter 3, Administration, Configuration and Management, reveals how to administer and configure RabbitMQ instances, how to install and manage RabbitMQ plugins, and how to use the various utilities provided as part of the RabbitMQ installation in order to accomplish a number of administrative tasks. A brief overview of the RabbitMQ management HTTP API is provided.

Chapter 4, Clustering, discusses what built-in clustering support is provided in the message broker and how it can be used to enable scalability in terms of message queues. A sample RabbitMQ cluster is created in order to demonstrate how nodes can be added/removed from a cluster and how RabbitMQ clients can connect to the cluster.

Chapter 5, High Availability, extends on the concepts of clustering by providing an overview of how a RabbitMQ cluster can be made more reliable in terms of mirrored queues and how messages can be replicated between remote instances using the Federation and Shovel plugins. High availability in terms of client connections and reliable delivery is also discussed with AMQP transactions, publisher confirms, and client reconnections.

Chapter 6, Integrations, provides you with a number of practical scenarios for integration of the message broker with the Spring framework, with ESB (enterprise services bus) systems such as MuleESB and WS02, and with database management systems (RDBMS and NoSQL). Deployment options for RabbitMQ using systems such as Puppet, Docker, and Vagrant are discussed in the chapter. A brief overview of how RabbitMQ applications can be tested using third-party frameworks is provided at the end of the chapter.

Chapter 7, Performance Monitoring and Tuning, gives a detailed list of factors that must be considered in terms of performance tuning of the message broker. The PerfTest tool is used to demonstrate how the RabbitMQ performance can be tested. At the end of the chapter, several monitoring solutions that provide support for RabbitMQ such as Nagios, Munin, and Monit are used to demonstrate how the message broker can be monitored in terms of stability and performance.

Chapter 8, Troubleshooting, illustrates a number of problems that can occur during the startup of the message broker and normal operation along with the various causes and resolutions in such cases. A brief primer on the Erlang programming language is provided for the purpose of understanding and analyzing the RabbitMQ crash dump—either directly or using the Crashdump Viewer for convenience.

Chapter 9, Security, provides a high-level overview of the vulnerability landscape related to the message broker along with a number of techniques to secure a RabbitMQ setup. Authentication, authorization, and secure communication are among the most important concepts covered in the chapter.

Chapter 10, Internals, discusses the internal architecture of the message broker and provides a detailed overview on the most important components that RabbitMQ comprises of.

Appendix A, Contributing to RabbitMQ, provides a short guide on how to get the RabbitMQ sources, how to set up a development environment, and how to build the message broker. A short discussion on how to contribute to the RabbitMQ ecosystem is provided as part of the appendix.

What you need for this book

In order to get the most out of this book, the reader is expected to have at least a basic understanding of what messaging is all about and a good understanding in at least one object-oriented programming language. As the book features the RabbitMQ Java client API in order to demonstrate how to use the message broker, it is good to have at least a basic understanding of the Java programming language. Most of the examples are not specific to a particular operating system; if they are, it is explicitly mentioned whether this is, for example, a Windows- or Unix-based distribution such as Ubuntu. For this reason, there is no particular requirement for an operating system in order to run the examples.

Who this book is for

If you are a developer or system administrator with basic knowledge in messaging who wants to learn RabbitMQ or further enhance your knowledge in working with the message broker, then this book is ideal for you. For a full understanding of some the examples in the book, basic knowledge of the Java programming language is required. Feeling comfortable with RabbitMQ is a great way to leverage your expertise in the world of messaging systems.

Conventions

In this book, you will find a number of text styles that distinguish between different kinds of information. Here are some examples of these styles and an explanation of their meaning.

Code words in text, names of third-party applications, utilities, folder names, filenames, file extensions andpathnames are shown in bold as follows: "We already saw how easy it is to `start/stop/restart` instances using the `rabbitmqctl` and `rabbitmq-server` utilities that are part of the standard RabbitMQ installation."

A block of code displayed in a box with console font:

```
<dependency>
 <groupId>log4j</groupId>
 <artifactId>log4j</artifactId>
 <version>1.2.16</version>
</dependency>
```

A block of configuration or output is also displayed in a box as follows:

```
sudo apt-get install rabbitmq-server -y
sudo rabbitmq-plugins enable rabbitmq_management
sudo service rabbitmq-server restart
```

New terms and **important words** are also shown in bold. Words that you see on the screen, for example, in menus or dialog boxes, appear in the text like this: "Clicking the **Next** button moves you to the next screen."

Reader feedback

Feedback from our readers is always welcome. Let us know what you think about this book—what you liked or disliked. Reader feedback is important for us as it helps us develop titles that you will really get the most out of.

To send us general feedback, simply e-mail feedback@packtpub.com, and mention the book's title in the subject of your message.

If there is a topic that you have expertise in and you are interested in either writing or contributing to a book, see our author guide at www.packtpub.com/authors.

Customer support

Now that you are the proud owner of a Packt book, we have a number of things to help you to get the most from your purchase.

Downloading the example code

You can download the example code files from your account at http://www.packtpub.com for all the Packt Publishing books you have purchased. If you purchased this book elsewhere, you can visit http://www.packtpub.com/support and register to have the files e-mailed directly to you.

Errata

Although we have taken every care to ensure the accuracy of our content, mistakes do happen. If you find a mistake in one of our books—maybe a mistake in the text or the code—we would be grateful if you could report this to us. By doing so, you can save other readers from frustration and help us improve subsequent versions of this book. If you find any errata, please report them by visiting http://www.packtpub.com/submit-errata, selecting your book, clicking on the **Errata Submission Form** link, and entering the details of your errata. Once your errata are verified, your submission will be accepted and the errata will be uploaded to our website or added to any list of existing errata under the Errata section of that title.

To view the previously submitted errata, go to https://www.packtpub.com/books/content/support and enter the name of the book in the search field. The required information will appear under the **Errata** section.

Piracy

Piracy of copyrighted material on the Internet is an ongoing problem across all media. At Packt, we take the protection of our copyright and licenses very seriously. If you come across any illegal copies of our works in any form on the Internet, please provide us with the location address or website name immediately so that we can pursue a remedy.

Please contact us at copyright@packtpub.com with a link to the suspected pirated material.

We appreciate your help in protecting our authors and our ability to bring you valuable content.

Questions

If you have a problem with any aspect of this book, you can contact us at questions@packtpub.com, and we will do our best to address the problem.

1
Introducing RabbitMQ

In the world of enterprise messaging systems there are a number of patterns and practices that are already successfully applied in order improve to scalability and interoperability between different components in a system or between varying in size and complexity systems. RabbitMQ is one such messaging solution, which combines powerful messaging capabilities with easy use and availability on a number of target platforms.

The following topics will be covered in this chapter:

- Fundamentals of enterprise messaging
- RabbitMQ brief overview
- RabbitMQ features
- Comparing RabbitMQ to other technologies
- Installing RabbitMQ

Enterprise messaging

A typical enterprise will have a number of systems that must typically communicate with each other in order to implement a well-defined business process. A question that is frequently tackled for this reason is how to implement the communication channel between these types of systems? For example, consider the following diagram:

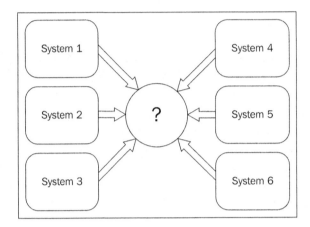

The question mark in the preceding picture denotes the communication media for the six systems that are illustrated. In the diagram, we can think of these separate systems as the components of one large system and the problem stays the same. Before discussing the various alternatives for integration, a number of key factors are considered, as follows:

- **Loose coupling**: At what degree do the different systems depend on each other or can operate independently?
- **Real-time workload processing**: How fast is the communication between the systems?
- **Scalability**: How does the entire system scale when more systems are added and the workload demands an increase?
- **Maintainability**: How hard it is to maintain the integrated systems?
- **Extensibility**: How easy it is to integrate new systems?

Let's assume that the systems communicate directly via some kind of remote procedure calls as shown in the following diagram:

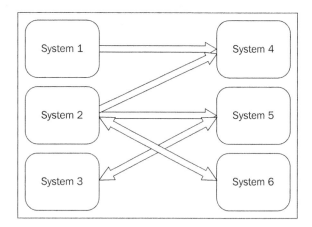

This implies that separate communication links must be established between each pair of systems, which leads to tight coupling, a lot of effort to maintain all of the links, reduced scalability, and reduced extensibility (for every new system that is added, a few more communication links with other systems must be created). However, real-time communication requirements might be met with some additional effort to design the communication links.

A second approach is to use a shared file system in order to exchange files between the systems that are being integrated, as illustrated in the following diagram:

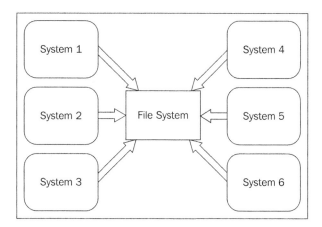

A shared file system is used to provide the communication medium. Each system may export data to a file that can be imported and used by other systems. The fact that each system may support its own data format leads to the fact that each system must have a particular mechanism to import data from every other system that it needs to communicate with. This, on other hand, leads to the same problems that are described in the case of direct communication. Moreover, real-time communication requirements might be more difficult to establish and reading or writing data from disk is also an expensive operation.

A third option is to use a shared database as shown in the following diagram:

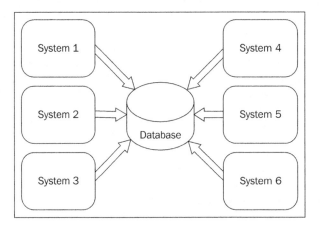

Here, all the systems should depend on the same database schema. Although this reduces coupling between systems and improves extensibility (new systems must conform to a single database schema in order to integrate with other systems), real-time workload processing is still an issue. Scalability and maintainability depend directly on the type of database that is being used and they could turn out to be weak factors especially if it is a relational database (this may not be the case if NoSQL solutions are applicable for the particular use case).

Messaging comes to the rescue when considering the problems that arise when applying the previous approaches. Consider the following diagram for the **Enterprise Messaging System**:

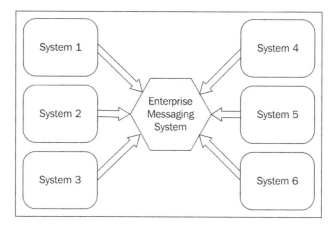

A message is the central unit of communication used in enterprise messaging systems. A message typically consists of the following:

- A message header: It provides metadata about the message such as encoding, routing information, and security-related information
- A message body: It provides the actual data that is carried by the message, represented in a proper format

The messaging system itself provides mechanisms to validate, store, route, and transform messages that are being sent between the different systems. Each system is responsible for crafting its own message that is transferred via the messaging system (also called the messaging broker) to other systems that are connected to the broker and configured to receive that particular type of message. Each system may create a message in a proper format that is specified by the protocol of the message broker — meaning that the system is only coupled with that particular protocol. If the broker implements a protocol that is based on a well-recognized standard, then this would further decouple the systems from that particular message broker implementation.

Real-time workload processing is typically quite fast as the particular protocol that is implemented by different messaging brokers is optimized to process message data in a reliable and secure manner with minimal overhead. Most messaging solutions provide a number of facilities that allow easy configuration, management, and monitoring; thus, simplifying maintainability. Clustering support is also considered by most implementations due to scalability and reliability requirements and increasing workload demands. Integrating new systems is a matter of implementing a mechanism for direct communication with the message broker.

In case the different systems provide different implementations of messaging protocols (such as REST, SOAP, JSON-RPC, JMX, AMQP, and many others), a messaging system could further provide various adapters for the different protocols as well as extended mechanisms for routing and transformation of different types of messages — this extended functionality also categorizes the message brokers as **Enterprise Service Bus (ESB)** solutions. One major drawback of an ESB is that it must implement all the communication requirements of all systems that are being integrated by the ESB, otherwise workarounds must be used in order to implement direct communication between the integrated systems (thus, neglecting the usage of an ESB).

Use cases

There are a variety of scenarios where messaging systems may be applied, such as the following:

- **Financial services**: High rate real-time trade transactions handled between different systems
- **Social networking**: Activity streams and event propagation between different components in a social network
- **E-mailing**: Sending e-mail notifications or digests periodically to a large number of users
- Processing large volumes of data upon request, such as image rendering
- Chat services
- Propagation of events throughout a system
- Any type of real-time system integration (system of systems)

As you can see, messaging solutions can be applied to a variety of scenarios that typically involve a number of systems that must communicate in a timely manner or perform a large number of time-consuming tasks. Messaging solutions are also extensively being deployed by Cloud providers in order to provide messaging as a service for Cloud-based applications.

Solutions

A wide variety of open source and property messaging solutions are available for use, which are based on the multitude of use cases. The choice of a messaging broker depends on a number of factors, as shown in the following:

- **Supporting tools, documentation and services**: These are tools for management and monitoring of the broker along with possible options to receive support, typically the support is guaranteed only for commercial brokers. For open source, this depends on the activeness of the community.

- **Ease of configuration**: This shows how easy it is to set up and configure the message broker.

- **Functionality**: The features implemented by the solution and their coverage of the usage scenario. Here the supported protocols for message transfer play a key role in the decision.

- The cost and licensing model.

Patterns

A messaging system provides patterns for communication between system endpoints.

Point-to-point

In a point-to-point communication model, there is exactly one sender and one receiver of a message. In case there are multiple senders that are applicable for the purpose of receiving the message, only one of them succeeds. Such receivers are also referred to as **competing consumers**, indicating that any of them are eligible to receive the message. The sender does not receive a response in a point-to-point model.

Publish-subscribe

In a Publish-subscribe communication model, there is one sender and multiple receivers (subscribers) of the message. It is a form of fire-and-forget, where the sender does not await for a response once the message is sent to the broker.

Request-response

In a request-response communication model, there is one sender and one receiver that sends a response to the sender of the message.

Understanding RabbitMQ

The RabbitMQ messaging server is an open source implementation of the **AMQP 0-9-1 protocol (Advanced Message Queuing Protocol)** that defines how messages should be queued, routed, and delivered in a reliable and secure manner. AMQP 1.0, which is an **OASIS (Organization for the Advancement of Structured Information Standards)**, is not directly supported in the message broker; however, RabbitMQ provides a plugin for AMQP 1.0 (as it is not backward-compatible with AMQP 0-9-1). OASIS is a non-profit organization that works for the development of a number of technology standards. As an open standard, AMQP promotes interoperability among the messaging brokers that implement the protocol. It also defines the delivery semantics for a message, which dictates how many times that message can be sent from one endpoint to another — zero or once, exactly once or multiple times. As a wire protocol, AMQP provides better performance in regard to other messaging protocols such as **XMPP (Extensible Messaging and Presence Protocol)**.

Before we discuss more about RabbitMQ as a message broker, we will introduce some terminologies from the RabbitMQ world that we will use frequently throughout the book:

- **exchanges**: These are the RabbitMQ server endpoints to which the clients will connect and send messages. Each endpoint is identified by a unique key.

- **queues**: These are the RabbitMQ server components that buffer messages coming from one or more exchanges and send them to the corresponding message receivers. The messages in a queue can also be offloaded to a persistent storage (such queues are also called **durable queues**) that provides a higher degree of reliability in case of a failed messaging server; once the server is running again, the messages from persistent storage are placed back in the corresponding queues for transfer to recipients. Each queue is identified by a unique key.

- **bindings**: These are the logical link between exchanges and queues. Each binding is a rule that specifies how the exchanges should route messages to queues. A binding may have a routing key that can be used by clients in order to specify the routing semantics of a message.

- **virtual hosts**: The logical units that divide RabbitMQ server components (such as exchanges, queues, and users) into separate groups for better administration and access control. Each AMQP client connection is bound to a concrete virtual host.

The AMQP protocol allows a client to establish a one-way logical link to send messages for exchange. Each logical link is a separate AMQP channel that may provide additional options for the reliable transfer of messages. In this regard, a single-client TCP connection to the RabbitMQ server allows multiple AMQP channels of communication. Since AMQP does not provide the capability to retrieve the list of queues, exchanges, or bindings that are defined in the RabbitMQ message broker, client applications must specify the exchange name, queue names, and, optionally, routing information by means of routing keys for particular bindings. AMQP is a programmatic protocol that allows its clients to create and delete exchanges, queues, and bindings when necessary. RabbitMQ addresses some limitations of AMQP by providing custom extensions apart from the fact that the AMQP protocol itself is extensible. In order to simply application development, RabbitMQ provides several exchange types out of the box, as follows:

- **direct exchange**: This delivers a message based on a routing key that is provided in the message header (bindings should already be defined between the direct exchange and the queue). There is a pre-created direct exchange with the name **.amq.direct**. A specialized type of a direct exchange called **default exchange** with the empty string as the exchange name is also pre-created in the message broker. It has the special property where the binding key that is specified by the client should match the name of the queue to which a message is routed.

- **fanout exchange**: This delivers a message to all the queues that are bound to the exchange; it can be used to establish a broadcast mechanism for the delivery of messages to the queues. There is a pre-created fanout exchange with name **.amq.fanout**.

- **topic exchange**: This delivers the message to queues based on a routing filter specified between the topic exchange and queues; it can be used to establish a multicast mechanism for the delivery of messages. There is a pre-created topic exchange with the name **.amq.topic**.

- **headers exchange**: This can be used to deliver messages to queues based on other message header attributes (and not the routing key). There are two pre-created headers exchanges with names **.amq.headers** and **.amq.match**.

Receivers can either subscribe to a queue in order to receive messages (also called **push-style** communication) or request messages on demand from a queue (also called **pull-style** communication).

Features

The RabbitMQ message broker provides a number of features and tools that support production-level deployment, management, and configuration of the RabbitMQ server instances as shown in the following:

- **support for multiple protocols**: Apart from AMQP, RabbitMQ provides support for the STOMP, MQTT, and HTTP protocols by the means of RabbitMQ plug-ins.

- **routing capabilities**: As we already saw, we can implement rules to route messages between exchanges and queues by means of bindings, moreover, more custom exchange types can be defined that can provide additional routing capabilities.

- **support for multiple programming languages**: There are a variety of supported clients for a great variety of programming languages.

- **reliable delivery**: This is a mechanism that guarantees successful message delivery by the means of acknowledgements. It can be enabled between the producer and the broker as well as the broker and the consumer.

- **clustering**: This provides a mechanism to implement scalable applications in terms of the RabbitMQ message broker.

- **federation**: This is an alternative mechanism to implement scalable applications with RabbitMQ by the means of transferring messages between exchanges and queues in different broker instances without the need to create a RabbitMQ cluster.

- **high availability**: This ensures that if a broker fails, communication will be redirected to a different broker instance. It is implemented by the means of mirroring queues; messages from a queue on a master broker instance are copied to a queue on a slave broker instance and, once the message is acknowledge, the messages are discarded from both the master and slave instances.

- **management and monitoring**: A number of utilities are built around the RabbitMQ broker server that provide these capabilities.

- **Authentication and access control**.

- **pluggable architecture**: RabbitMQ provides a mechanism to extend its functionality by the means of RabbitMQ plug-ins.

All of these features will be covered in detail in the next chapters.

Comparison with other technologies

As RabbitMQ is not the only player in the world of enterprise messaging solutions, it is good to see what makes RabbitMQ different compared to other messaging systems. A short list of alternative solutions (some of them also implementing the AMQP protocol) may include systems such as Apache ActiveMQ, Apache Kafka, Apache Qpid, JBoss Messaging, Microsoft BizTalk Server, and WebSphere Message Broker. There are different benchmarks that can be found throughout the internet that show us the relative results in comparison to the different types of brokers in terms of message sending (from publisher to broker) and message delivery (from broker to consumer). In case you need to compare RabbitMQ with the previously mentioned or other messaging solutions, you can apply the following strategy:

- Select a subset of technologies that are suitable for your use case based on the variety of factors that are listed at the beginning of this chapter

- Perform different types of benchmark based on the variations of size and number of messages that will be sent for the purpose of processing by each solution in the comparison group, based on the format of messages for the particular use case

Installation

You can download a RabbitMQ distribution package for the operating system of your choice from `http://www.rabbitmq.com/Windows`.

For Windows operating systems, you have the ability to use the provided RabbitMQ installer (the simpler alternative) or manually install the broker using the provided zip distribution archive (requires additional setup of Windows system paths). We will provide an overview of the installation process for Windows 7 using the installer for Rabbit 3.3.5 (`rabbitmq-server-3.3.5.exe`) that is quite straight-forward. Initially, the installer checks whether Erlang is installed on the target Windows system and, if it cannot find it, a dialog prompts you to install it, as shown in the following image:

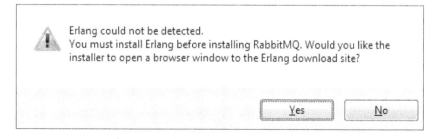

If you click **Yes**, the dialog redirects you to the official Erlang website. There, you will find the appropriate binaries for your 32-bit/64-bit Windows operating system. Download and install the Erlang 17.3 distribution (compatible with RabbitMQ 3.3.5) for 64-bit Windows (`otp_win64_17.3.exe`):

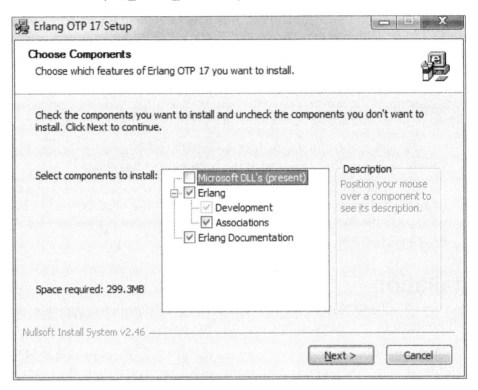

File associations can be established and the Erlang documentation can be installed as a part of the Erlang installation process:

The next step is to specify the location to install Erlang:

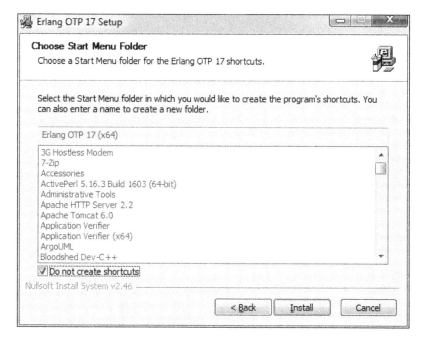

Finally, you have the option to place an Erlang shortcut in the Start menu folder. After the installation is finished, you can run the RabbitMQ 3.3.5 server installer again:

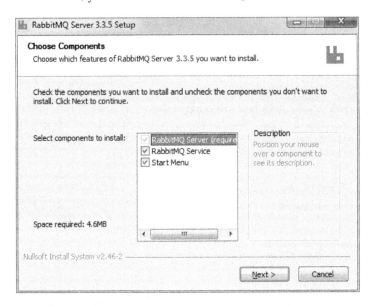

You can specify in addition that Start menu items and a Windows service should be added along with RabbitMQ server installation. Adding a Windows service for RabbitMQ server is usually recommended as it provides a convenient mechanism to manage a RabbitMQ server instance:

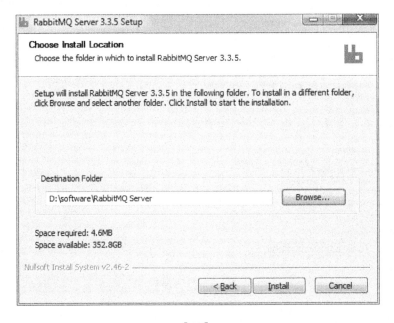

The final step is to specify the location to install the RabbitMQ server. Once the installation is complete, the installer tries to start the RabbitMQ server and, if your Windows firewall is turned on, you might be prompted to allow access to the RabbitMQ server in order to open a port on the target machine (the default port is 5672 for a RabbitMQ server node instance). In order to check whether the RabbitMQ service is running, you can open `services.msc` from the Windows **Run** menu and check whether the **RabbitMQ** service has started. Additionally, you can check whether the RabbitMQ instance node is initiated, by default on port 5672, by executing from the command prompt:

```
netstat -a
```

RabbitMQ installation also provides a number of command-line utilities that you can use in order to manage the RabbitMQ instance, which is located under the `rabbitmq_server-3.3.5\sbin` folder in the RabbitMQ installation directory. You can use the `rabbitmqctl` utility to check the status of a broker, start, or stop it:

```
rabbitmqctl.bat status
rabbitmqctl.bat stop
rabbitmqctl.bat start
```

In addition to this, rabbitmqctl provides a number of other commands that can be used to manage the RabbitMQ broker. There is a RabbitMQ management plugin that provides the ability to manage a RabbitMQ broker from a web-based interface and in particular to do the following:

- Manage broker objects such as message queues, users, and permissions
- Send messages to the broker
- Receive messages from the broker
- Monitor and manage connections to the broker
- Monitor broker workload
- Monitor resource usage such as memory, processes, and file descriptors that are used by the broker

These are included in the set of plugins that are installed by default; however, it must be enabled by executing the rabbitmq-plugins utility that is located under the `rabbitmq_server-3.3.5\sbin` folder in the RabbitMQ installation directory from the following command prompt:

```
rabbitmq-plugins.bat enable rabbitmq_management
```

After the management plugin is enabled, you have to restart the RabbitMQ server:

```
rabbitmq-server.bat restart
```

The management plugin starts an http server, on port 15672, by default in order to verify that the plugin is trying to open http://localhost:15672/ from a browser. You will be prompted to provide a **Username** and **Password** in order to login:

By default, RabbitMQ installs with a user with a guest name and guest password that are only available from local host connections to the broker. In the next chapter, we will see how to manage users for a RabbitMQ server.

Linux

For various Linux distributions, there are out-of-the-box packages provided for the RabbitMQ server. Some Linux distributions also provide you with the ability to install the broker directly from a package repository. We will provide an overview of the installation process for Ubuntu 12.04 Desktop edition based on a package repository that we can also download and install directly, a RabbitMQ Debian package for the purpose. To install the broker and enable the management plugin, open a terminal and execute the following command:

```
echo "deb http://www.rabbitmq.com/debian/ testing main"  | sudo tee  /
etc/apt/sources.list.d/rabbitmq.list > /dev/null
sudo wget http://www.rabbitmq.com/rabbitmq-signing-key-public.asc
sudo apt-key add rabbitmq-signing-key-public.asc
sudo apt-get update
sudo apt-get install rabbitmq-server -y
sudo rabbitmq-plugins enable rabbitmq_management
sudo service rabbitmq-server restart
```

The server installation also installs utilities for the management of the RabbitMQ server—used in the same way as in the Windows installation of RabbitMQ.

Case study: CSN (Corporate Social Network)

The **Corporate Social Network (CSN)** is a social networking service that is being deployed in an enterprise and allows its users to upload content and interact with each other. In particular, the system allows the user to post blogs, upload files, subscribe to other user profiles (in order to track the activity of other users), and chat with other users. The social network uses RabbitMQ in order to process events that have been triggered by user activity, trigger long-running jobs (such as batch file uploading), and serve as a backbone for the delivery of chat messages from the chat feature of the social network. The following diagram provides a high-level overview of the components of the system:

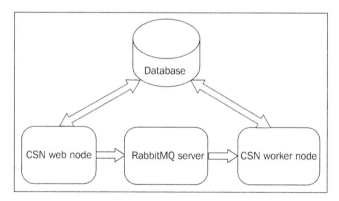

We will design the system from the very beginning and then start expanding it. In the meantime, we will demonstrate the various capabilities of RabbitMQ by applying them to the extensions of the social network.

Summary

In this chapter, we covered the fundamentals of enterprise messaging solutions and discussed the features of RabbitMQ along with the installation process. A brief comparison with other messaging brokers was provided in order to reveal what the strengths and weaknesses of RabbitMQ are compared to the other alternatives. We also introduced a case study project CSN that makes use of RabbitMQ as a messaging solution for propagation of events throughout the system and lays the basis for further demonstrations on the various features of RabbitMQ.

Exercises

Attempt the following questions:

1. What is messaging?

2. What are the typical components of a message broker?

3. What appropriate usage scenarios can you think of for the application of messaging systems?

4. Which message patterns does RabbitMQ support and how?

5. What are the advantages of using AMQP for messaging compared to other protocols?

6. What are the different features that are supported by RabbitMQ?

7. What are the prerequisites for RabbitMQ installation on a target operating system?

2

Design Patterns with RabbitMQ

As a robust messaging solution, RabbitMQ provides different utilities for distributing messages between endpoints in the communication channel. These utilities provide an implementation of best practices and design patterns that apply to messaging solutions and form the backbone of a messaging broker such as RabbitMQ.

Topics covered in the chapter:

- Messaging patterns in RabbitMQ
- Point-to-point communication
- Publish-subscribe communication
- Request-reply communication
- Message router

Messaging patterns in RabbitMQ

Messaging patterns in RabbitMQ are implemented based on exchanges, queues, and the bindings between them. We can distinguish between the different approaches for implementing a design pattern with RabbitMQ:

- For point-to-point communication between the publisher and the broker you can use a default or a direct exchange in order to deliver a message to a single queue. However, note that there might be multiple subscribers to this single queue, thus implementing publish-subscribe between the broker and the message receivers bound to that queue.

- For publish-subscribe, we can use a fanout exchange, which will deliver a message from an exchange to all queues that are bound to this exchange; in this manner, we may have a queue-per-subscriber strategy for implementing publish-subscribe.

- For request-response communication, we can use two separate exchanges and two queues; the publisher sets a message identifier in the message header and sends the request message to the request exchange, which in turn delivers the message to the request queue. The subscriber retrieves the message from the request queue, processes it, and sends a response message to the response exchange by also setting the same message identifier found in the request message to the response message header. The response exchange then delivers the message to a response queue. The publisher is subscribed to a response queue in order to retrieve response messages and uses the message identifier from the response message header to map the response message to the corresponding request message.

- For message routing we can use a `topic` exchange in order to deliver messages based on a binding key pattern or a `headers` exchange based on one or more headers.

It is important to remember that AMQP 0-9-1 protocol messages are load-balanced between consumers in a round-robin fashion. In this case, if there are multiple consumers on a message queue (bound using the `basic.consume` AMQP protocol command) then only one of them will receive the message, signifying that we have competing consumers. The same applies for the `basic.get` AMQP protocol command that retrieves a message from a queue on-demand (pull style) rather than by consumption (push style). If a message arrives on a queue that has no subscribers then the message will stay in the queue until a new subscriber is bound to the queue or the message is explicitly requested using `basic.get`. A message can also be rejected using the `basic.reject` AMQP protocol command. We will illustrate each of the preceding message patterns with concrete examples in subsequent sections. Before trying out the examples, you have to include the AMQP client library for Java. If you are using Maven, you can include the following dependencies for the client library along with the `slf4j` dependencies that provide the slf4j logging features used to provide logging capabilities in the examples:

```
<dependency>
    <groupId>com.rabbitmq</groupId>
    <artifactId>amqp-client</artifactId>
    <version>3.4.1</version>
</dependency>
<dependency>
    <groupId>org.slf4j</groupId>
    <artifactId>slf4j-api</artifactId>
```

```
        <version>1.6.1</version>
    </dependency>
    <dependency>
        <groupId>org.slf4j</groupId>
        <artifactId>slf4j-log4j12</artifactId>
        <version>1.6.1</version>
    </dependency>
    <dependency>
        <groupId>log4j</groupId>
        <artifactId>log4j</artifactId>
        <version>1.2.16</version>
    </dependency>
```

In order to send messages to RabbitMQ, the `Sender` class will be used:

```java
import java.io.IOException;

import org.slf4j.Logger;
import org.slf4j.LoggerFactory;

import com.rabbitmq.client.ConnectionFactory;
import com.rabbitmq.client.Connection;
import com.rabbitmq.client.Channel;

public class Sender {

    private final static String QUEUE_NAME = "event_queue";
    private final static Logger LOGGER =
        LoggerFactory.getLogger(Sender.class);
    private static final String DEFAULT_EXCHANGE = "";
    private Channel channel;
    private Connection connection;
}
```

The `initialize()` method is used to initialize the message sender by doing the following:

- Creating a `ConnectionFactory` that is used to create AMQP connections to a running RabbitMQ server instance; in this case, this is an instance running on localhost and accepting connections on the default port (5672)

- Creating a new connection using the connection factory

- Creating a new channel for sending messages in the created connection:

```
public void initialize() {
    try {
        ConnectionFactory factory = new ConnectionFactory();
        factory.setHost("localhost");
        connection = factory.newConnection();
        channel = connection.createChannel();
    } catch (IOException e) {
        LOGGER.error(e.getMessage(), e);
    }
}
```

The `send()` method has two variants: one that accepts a message and sends it to the default queue and a second one that accepts an exchange name, exchange type, and the message to send. The first variant is appropriate for point-to-point communication and does the following:

- Declares a queue in the message broker using the `queueDeclare()` method; if the queue is already created then it is not recreated by the method
- Publishes a message on the default exchange that is delivered to that queue

The second variant of `send()` is appropriate for the publish-subscribe type of communication and does the following:

- Declares the specified exchange along with its type on the message bus using the `exchangeDeclare()` method; the exchange is not recreated if it exists on the message bus
- Sends a message to this exchange with a routing key equal to the empty string (we are indicating that we will not use the routing key with this variant of the method):

```
public void send(String message) {
    try {
        channel.queueDeclare(QUEUE_NAME, false, false, false,
null);
        channel.basicPublish(DEFAULT_EXCHANGE, QUEUE_NAME,
null,
            message.getBytes());
    } catch (IOException e) {
        LOGGER.error(e.getMessage(), e);
    }
}

public void send(String exchange, String type, String message)
{
```

```
    try {
        channel.exchangeDeclare(exchange, type);
        channel.basicPublish(exchange, "", null,
                message.getBytes());
    } catch (IOException e) {
        LOGGER.error(e.getMessage(), e);
    }
}
```

The destroy() method is used to close the connection and all connection channels to the message broker:

```
public void destroy() {
    try {
        if (connection != null) {
            connection.close();
        }
    } catch (IOException e) {
        LOGGER.warn(e.getMessage(), e);
    }
}
}
```

Point-to-point communication

The following diagram provides an overview of the scenario that we will implement:

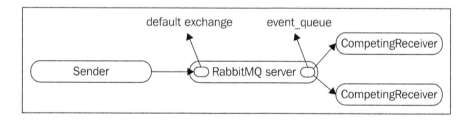

For point-to-point communication, the sender can use either the default exchange or a direct exchange (that uses the routing key to determine to which queue a message must be sent; the routing key should match the binding key between the exchange and the queue). The CompetingReceiver class can be used to subscribe to a particular queue and receive messages from that queue:

```
import java.io.IOException;
import org.slf4j.Logger;
```

```java
import org.slf4j.LoggerFactory;
import com.rabbitmq.client.Channel;
import com.rabbitmq.client.Connection;
import com.rabbitmq.client.ConnectionFactory;
import com.rabbitmq.client.ConsumerCancelledException;
import com.rabbitmq.client.QueueingConsumer;
import com.rabbitmq.client.ShutdownSignalException;

public class CompetingReceiver {

    private final static String QUEUE_NAME = "event_queue";
    private final static Logger LOGGER =
LoggerFactory.getLogger(Sender.class);
    private Connection connection = null;
    private Channel channel = null;
    public void initialize() {
        try {
            ConnectionFactory factory =
new ConnectionFactory();
            factory.setHost("localhost");
            connection = factory.newConnection();
            channel = connection.createChannel();
        } catch (IOException e) {
            LOGGER.error(e.getMessage(), e);
        }
    }
}
```

The `receive()` method is used to receive a message from the queue named event_queue by doing the following:

- Creating the event_queue in the message broker, if not already created, using the `queueDeclare()` method

- Creating a `QueueingConsumer` instance that is used as the handler for messages from the event_queue queue

- Registering the QueueingConsumer as a message consumer using the basicConsume() method of the Channel instance that represents the AMQP channel to the message broker

- Consuming a message from the event_queue queue using the nextDeliver() method of the QueueingConsumer instance, which blocks until a message arrives on the queue; QueueingConsumer.Delivery represents the received message:

```
public String receive() {
    if (channel == null) {
        initialize();
    }
    String message = null;
    try {
        channel.queueDeclare(QUEUE_NAME, false, false, false,
null);
        QueueingConsumer consumer =
new QueueingConsumer(channel);
        channel.basicConsume(QUEUE_NAME, true,
consumer);
        QueueingConsumer.Delivery delivery =
consumer.nextDelivery();
        message = new String(delivery.getBody());
        LOGGER.info("Message received: " + message);
        return message;

    } catch (IOException e) {
        LOGGER.error(e.getMessage(), e);
    } catch (ShutdownSignalException e) {
        LOGGER.error(e.getMessage(), e);
    } catch (ConsumerCancelledException e) {
        LOGGER.error(e.getMessage(), e);
    } catch (InterruptedException e) {
        LOGGER.error(e.getMessage(), e);
    }
    return message;
}
```

The destroy() method closes the AMQP connection and must be called explicitly when needed; closing the connection closes all AMQP channels created in that connection:

```
public void destroy() {
    if (connection != null) {
        try {
            connection.close();
        } catch (IOException e) {
            LOGGER.warn(e.getMessage(), e);
        }
    }
}
```

In order to demonstrate the usage of the CompetingConsumer class in a point-to-point channel, we can use the DefaultExchangeSenderDemo class to send a message to the default exchange:

```
public class DefaultExchangeSenderDemo {

    public static void sendToDefaultExchange() {
        Sender sender = new Sender();
        sender.initialize();
        sender.send("Test message.");
        sender.destroy();
    }

    public static void main(String[] args) {
        sendToDefaultExchange();
    }
}
```

When invoking the `main()` method, a message is sent to the RabbitMQ server instance running on localhost; if no instance is running then a `java.net.ConnectionException` is thrown from the client. Assuming that there are no defined queues yet in the message broker, if you open the RabbitMQ management console you will notice the following before invoking the `main()` method:

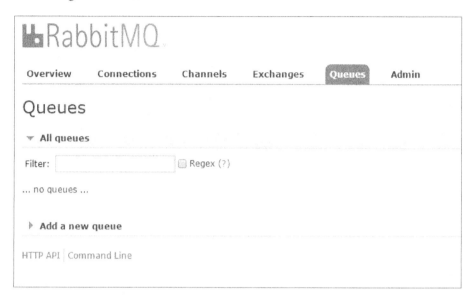

After invoking the `main()` method, you will notice that the `event_queue` is created:

Moreover, there is one unprocessed message in the queue; the Ready section gives the number of unprocessed messages on the particular queue. In order to consume the message CompetingReceiverDemo class, perform the following:

```java
public class CompetingReceiverDemo {

    public static void main(String[] args)
throws InterruptedException {
        final CompetingReceiver receiver1 = new CompetingReceiver();
        receiver1.initialize();
        final CompetingReceiver receiver2 = new CompetingReceiver();
        receiver2.initialize();

        Thread t1 = new Thread(new Runnable() {
            public void run() {
                receiver1.receive();
            }
        });
        Thread t2 = new Thread(new Runnable() {
            public void run() {
                receiver2.receive();
            }
        });
        t1.start();
        t2.start();
        t1.join();
        t2.join();
        receiver1.destroy();
        receiver2.destroy();
    }
}
```

We create two CompetingReceiver instances and invoke the receive() methods of the two instances in separate threads so that we have two subscribers for the same queue waiting for a message. The two threads are joined to the main application thread so that method execution continues once both consumers receive a message from the queue. Since our queue already has one message, one of the two consumers will receive the message while the other will continue to wait for a message. If we invoke the main() method of the DefaultExchangeSenderDemo class once again, the other consumer will also receive a message from the queue and the main() method of CompetingReceiverDemo() will terminate.

Publish-subscribe communication

The following diagram provides an overview of the scenario that we will implement:

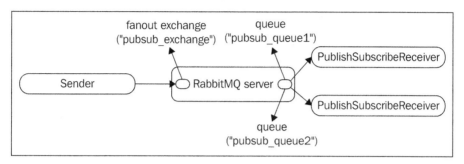

For publish-subscribers we can use a fanout exchange and bind any number of queues to that exchange regardless of the binding key. The PublishSubscribeReceiver class can be used to bind a specified queue to a fanout exchange and receive messages from it:

```
import java.io.IOException;
import org.slf4j.Logger;
import org.slf4j.LoggerFactory;
import com.rabbitmq.client.Channel;
import com.rabbitmq.client.Connection;
import com.rabbitmq.client.ConnectionFactory;
import com.rabbitmq.client.ConsumerCancelledException;
import com.rabbitmq.client.QueueingConsumer;
import com.rabbitmq.client.ShutdownSignalException;

public class PublishSubscribeReceiver {

    private final static String EXCHANGE_NAME = "pubsub_exchange";
    private final static Logger LOGGER =
LoggerFactory.getLogger(Sender.class);
    private Channel channel = null;
    private Connection connection = null;

    public void initialize() {
        try {
            ConnectionFactory factory = new ConnectionFactory();
            factory.setHost("localhost");
            connection = factory.newConnection();
```

```
            channel = connection.createChannel();
        } catch (IOException e) {
            LOGGER.error(e.getMessage(), e);
        }
    }
    . . .
}
```

The `receive()` method can be used to retrieve a message from a queue that is bound to the `pubsub_exchange` fanout exchange and does the following:

- Creates the `pubsub_exchange`, if not already created
- Creates the specified queue if not already created
- Binds the queue to the `pubsub_exchange` using the `queueBind()` method of the Channel instance that represents the AMQP channel for the receiver; notice that in this case we don't specify any particular binding key and for that reason we are using the empty string
- Creates a new `QueueingConsumer` instance, registered using the AMQP channel, and the `nextDelivery()` method is called to receive a message from the `channel`:

```
public String receive(String queue) {

    if (channel == null) {
        initialize();
    }

    String message = null;
    try {
        channel.exchangeDeclare(EXCHANGE_NAME, "fanout");
        channel.queueDeclare(queue, false, false, false, null);
        channel.queueBind(queue, EXCHANGE_NAME, "");
        QueueingConsumer consumer = new
QueueingConsumer(channel);
        channel.basicConsume(queue, true, consumer);
        QueueingConsumer.Delivery delivery =
consumer.nextDelivery();
        message = new String(delivery.getBody());
        LOGGER.info("Message received: " + message);
        return message;

    } catch (IOException e) {
```

```
                    LOGGER.error(e.getMessage(), e);
        } catch (ShutdownSignalException e) {
            LOGGER.error(e.getMessage(), e);
        } catch (ConsumerCancelledException e) {
            LOGGER.error(e.getMessage(), e);
        } catch (InterruptedException e) {
            LOGGER.error(e.getMessage(), e);
        }
        return message;
    }
```

And we also have a destroy() method:

```
    public void destroy() {
        try {
            if (connection != null) {
                connection.close();
            }
        } catch (IOException e) {
            LOGGER.warn(e.getMessage(), e);
        }
    }
}
```

In order to demonstrate the usage of QueueingConsumer for establishing a publish-subscribe communication channel, we will use the FanoutExchangeSenderDemo class to send a message to the pubsub_exchange fanout exchange:

```
public class FanoutExchangeSenderDemo {

    private static final String FANOUT_EXCHANGE_TYPE = "fanout";

    public static void sendToFanoutExchange(String exchange) {
        Sender sender = new Sender();
        sender.initialize();
        sender.send(exchange, FANOUT_EXCHANGE_TYPE, "Test message.");
        sender.destroy();
    }

    public static void main(String[] args) {
        sendToFanoutExchange("pubsub_exchange");
    }
}
```

When you invoke the `main()` method of the `FanoutExchangeSenderDemo` class, you may notice from the management console that the `pubsub_exchange` exchange is created in the RabbitMQ server instance separate from the predefined exchanges:

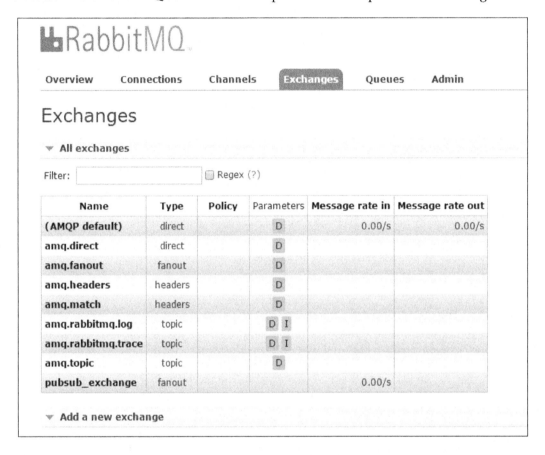

If you restart the RabbitMQ instance then you will not see the `pubsub_exchange` from the management console again, because the exchange is not marked as durable. In order to mark a queue/exchange as durable, you can provide an additional parameter to the `queueDeclare()`/`exchangeDeclare()` methods of the `Channel` class. In order to provide further message delivery guarantees on the broker, you can use the publisher confirms of the extension.

The PublishSubscribeReceiverDemo class provides a demonstration of the
PublishSubscribeReceiver class for the establishment of a publish-subscribe
channel:

```
public class PublishSubscribeReceiverDemo {

    public static void main(String[] args)
throws InterruptedException {
        final PublishSubscribeReceiver receiver1 =
new PublishSubscribeReceiver();
        receiver1.initialize();
        final PublishSubscribeReceiver receiver2 =
new PublishSubscribeReceiver();
        receiver2.initialize();
        Thread t1 = new Thread(new Runnable() {
            public void run() {
                receiver1.receive("pubsub_queue1");
            }
        });
        Thread t2 = new Thread(new Runnable() {
            public void run() {
                receiver2.receive("pubsub_queue2");
            }
        });
        t1.start();
        t2.start();
        t1.join();
        t2.join();

        receiver1.destroy();
        receiver2.destroy();
    }
}
```

The main() method creates two receivers that bind to two different queues:
pubsub_queue1 and pubsub_queue2. If you have already sent a message to the
pubsub_exchange exchange, it will be delivered to both queues and thus sent to
both consumers.

Request-reply communication

The following diagram provides an overview of the scenario that we will implement:

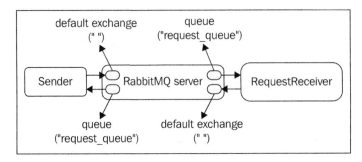

The sender will send a message to the default exchange with a routing key that matches the name of the designated request queue. The request receiver is a subscriber to the request queue. After a request message is received, the request receiver retrieves the value of the replyTo property from the message header, creates a response message, and sends it to the default exchange with a routing key that matches the replyTo property. This means that the replyTo property points to a queue that handles response messages and the sender is subscribed to that queue in order to receive a response.

Let's extend our Sender class with the following sendRequest() method, which sends a message to the request_exchange exchange, and the receiveResponse() method, which receives a message from the response_queue queue as follows:

```
private static final String REQUEST_QUEUE = "request_queue";
private static final String RESPONSE_QUEUE = "response_queue";
public void sendRequest(String requestQueue, String message, String
correlationId) {
    try {
        channel.queueDeclare(REQUEST_QUEUE, false, false, false,
null);
        channel.queueDeclare(RESPONSE_QUEUE, false, false, false,
null);
        AMQP.BasicProperties amqpProps = new AMQP.BasicProperties();
        amqpProps = amqpProps.builder()
            .correlationId(String.valueOf(correlationId))
            .replyTo(RESPONSE_QUEUE).build();
        channel.basicPublish(DEFAULT_EXCHANGE,
REQUEST_QUEUE, amqpProps,                              message.
getBytes());
    } catch (IOException e) {
```

```
            LOGGER.error(e.getMessage(), e);
        }
    }


    public String waitForResponse(final String correlationId) {
        QueueingConsumer consumer = new QueueingConsumer(channel);
        String result = null;

        try {
            channel.basicConsume(RESPONSE_QUEUE, true, consumer);
            QueueingConsumer.Delivery delivery = consumer.
    nextDelivery(3000);
            String message = new String(delivery.getBody());
            if (delivery.getProperties() != null) {
                String msgCorrelationId = delivery.getProperties()
                    .getCorrelationId();
                if (!correlationId.equals(msgCorrelationId)) {
                LOGGER.warn("Received response of another request.");
                } else {
                    result = message;
                }
            }
                                                    LOGGER.
    info("Message received: " + message);

        } catch (IOException e) {
            LOGGER.error(e.getMessage(), e);
        } catch (ShutdownSignalException e) {
            LOGGER.error(e.getMessage(), e);
        } catch (ConsumerCancelledException e) {
            LOGGER.error(e.getMessage(), e);
        } catch (InterruptedException e) {
            LOGGER.error(e.getMessage(), e);
        }
        return result;
    }
```

The sendRequest() method crafts an AMQP.BasicProperties instance and provides the replyTo and correlationId properties. The correlationId must be a unique identifier that is passed back in the response message and can be used by the sender to determine the request for which a response is received.

The `RequestReceiver` class provides a sample implementation of a request receiver:

```
public class RequestReceiver {

    private static final String DEFAULT_QUEUE = "";
    private static final String REQUEST_QUEUE = "request_queue";
    private final static Logger LOGGER =
      LoggerFactory.getLogger(Sender.class);
    private Connection connection = null;
    private Channel channel = null;

    public void initialize() {
        try {
            ConnectionFactory factory =
new ConnectionFactory();
            factory.setHost("localhost");
            connection = factory.newConnection();
            channel = connection.createChannel();
        } catch (IOException e) {
            LOGGER.error(e.getMessage(), e);
        }
    }
    . . .
}
```

The `receive()` method is used to read a request message from a queue:

```
public void receive() {

    if (channel == null) {
        initialize();
    }

    String message = null;
    try {
        channel.queueDeclare(REQUEST_QUEUE, false,
false, false, null);
        QueueingConsumer consumer = new QueueingConsumer(channel);
        channel.basicConsume(REQUEST_QUEUE, true, consumer);
        QueueingConsumer.Delivery delivery =
consumer.nextDelivery();
        message = new String(delivery.getBody());
```

```
        LOGGER.info("Request received: " + message);

        // do something with the request message ...

        BasicProperties properties = delivery.getProperties();
        if (properties != null) {
            AMQP.BasicProperties amqpProps =
new AMQP.BasicProperties();
            amqpProps = amqpProps.builder().correlationId(

String.valueOf(properties.getCorrelationId())).build();

            channel.basicPublish(DEFAULT_QUEUE,
properties.getReplyTo(), amqpProps, "Response message.".getBytes());
        } else {
            LOGGER.warn("Cannot determine response
destination for message.");
        }

    } catch (IOException e) {
        LOGGER.error(e.getMessage(), e);
    } catch (ShutdownSignalException e) {
        LOGGER.error(e.getMessage(), e);
    } catch (ConsumerCancelledException e) {
        LOGGER.error(e.getMessage(), e);
    } catch (InterruptedException e) {
        LOGGER.error(e.getMessage(), e);
    }
}
```

And again we have a destroy() method – it is important to make sure that you close your connections to the broker if you are no longer using them:

```
public void destroy() {
    if (connection != null) {
        try {
            connection.close();
        } catch (IOException e) {
            LOGGER.warn(e.getMessage(), e);
        }
    }
}
}
```

In order to send a request message we can use the `RequestSenderDemo` class:

```
public class RequestSenderDemo {

    private static final String REQUEST_QUEUE =
"request_queue";

    public static String sendToRequestReplyQueue() {
        Sender sender = new Sender();
        sender.initialize();
        sender.sendRequest(REQUEST_QUEUE, "Test message.", "MSG1");
        String result = sender.waitForResponse("MSG1");
        sender.destroy();
        return result;
    }
    public static void main(String[] args) {
        sendToRequestReplyQueue();
    }
}
```

In order to receive the request message and send a response message, you can use the `RequestReceiverDemo` class:

```
public class RequestReceiverDemo {

    public static void main(String[] args) throws InterruptedException
    {
        final RequestReceiver receiver = new RequestReceiver();
        receiver.initialize();
        receiver.receive();
        receiver.destroy();
    }
}
```

Message router

The following diagram provides an overview of the scenario that we will implement:

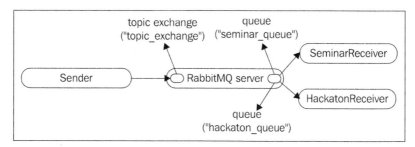

Let's say we have a service that triggers an event upon the creation of a new programming seminar, or hackathon, for a given community. We want to send all seminar events to a particular destination receiver and all hackaton events to another destination receiver. Moreover, we want to send messages to the same exchange. For that setup, a topic exchange is a rational choice; one queue will be bound to the topic exchange with the `seminar.#` routing key and another queue will be bound with `hackaton.#` routing key. The # character is special and serves as a pattern that matches any character sequence.

We can implement this type of message sending by further extending our Sender class:

```
private static final String SEMINAR_QUEUE = "seminar_queue";
private static final String HACKATON_QUEUE = "hackaton_queue";
private static final String TOPIC_EXCHANGE = "topic_exchange";

public void sendEvent(String exchange, String message, String
messageKey) {
    try {
        channel.exchangeDeclare(TOPIC_EXCHANGE, "topic");
        channel.queueDeclare(SEMINAR_QUEUE, false, false,
false, null);
        channel.queueDeclare(HACKATON_QUEUE, false, false,
false, null);
        channel.queueBind(SEMINAR_QUEUE, TOPIC_EXCHANGE,
"seminar.#");
        channel.queueBind(HACKATON_QUEUE, TOPIC_EXCHANGE,
"hackaton.#");
channel.basicPublish(TOPIC_EXCHANGE, messageKey, null,
```

```
        message.getBytes());
    } catch (IOException e) {
        LOGGER.error(e.getMessage(), e);
    }
}
```

In order to demonstrate event sending, we can use the `TopicSenderDemo` class:

```
public class TopicSenderDemo {

    private static final String TOPIC_EXCHANGE =
"topic_exchange";

    public static void sendToTopicExchange() {
        Sender sender = new Sender();
        sender.initialize();
        sender.sendEvent(TOPIC_EXCHANGE, "Test message 1.",
"seminar.java");
        sender.sendEvent(TOPIC_EXCHANGE, "Test message 2.",
"seminar.rabbitmq");
        sender.sendEvent(TOPIC_EXCHANGE, "Test message 3.",
"hackaton.rabbitmq");
        sender.destroy();
    }

    public static void main(String[] args) {
        sendToTopicExchange();
    }
}
```

Case study: Initial design of the CSN

The following diagram extends the general overview of a CSN in regard to a client browser that provides client-side interaction with the system:

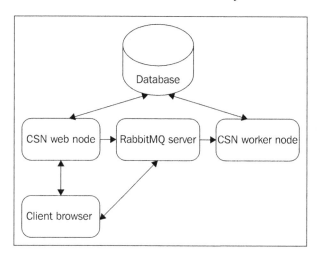

Now that we have seen how to implement messaging patterns in RabbitMQ, we can apply this to implement the following:

- Global event handling; we can use the default exchange along with a single queue called event_queue. The worker nodes as illustrated in the preceding diagram will subscribe to the event_queue and start handling events for long-running tasks in a round-robin fashion; the CompetingReceiver class is a proper alternative for the implementation of a point-to-point receiver on the worker nodes.

- Chat service; each user of the system will have a separate queue that will receive messages for that queue. You can use a variant—a point-to-point channel—to send a message from one user to the other. For group chatting, you can have a fanout or topic exchange (based on the implementation strategy) for the particular group that will be used to deliver messages to all use queues.

To implement a chat client that is displayed in the client's browser you have a number of alternatives, such as:

- Using the WebSocket protocol, since it allows two-way communication between the browser and the CSN frontend server; the frontend server sends the message to the RabbitMQ server for further handling. In this case, you may need to create a mapping between the WebSocket endpoints and AMQP queues.

- Implementing a browser plugin that makes use of the AMQP protocol directly; this allows you to connect clients directly to the RabbitMQ broker.

- Ajax requests with long polling; this option is not preferred since it implies a heavy footprint on network bandwidth but it is still another alternative.

Summary

In this chapter, we saw how to implement various messaging patterns in RabbitMQ. We also discussed how to design the various components of a **CSN** (**Corporate Social Network**) that makes use of such messaging patterns, with RabbitMQ as the message broker used in the system. In the next chapter we will see how to configure and administer RabbitMQ.

Exercises

1. How can you implement different enterprise integration patterns with RabbitMQ other than the ones listed in this chapter? Refer to the book *Enterprise Integration Patterns* by *Gregor Hohpe* and *Bobby Woolf*.

2. Can you think of any non-standard applications of RabbitMQ in CSN? List them and think of a general design for implementing them in CSN.

Administration, Configuration, and Management

3

In order to get the most out of a system, you need to know how to configure and control it. Depending on the type of system, these tasks could turn out to be quite daunting and onerous (consider a relational database, for example). However, the RabbitMQ team has provided very convenient facilities for administering and managing the message broker.

Topics covered in the chapter:

- Administering RabbitMQ instances
- Administering the RabbitMQ database
- Installing RabbitMQ plugins
- Configuring RabbitMQ instances
- Managing RabbitMQ instances
- Upgrading RabbitMQ

Administering RabbitMQ instances

Administration of RabbitMQ server instances can be considered in several directions:

- Starting/stopping/restarting instances
- Adding/removing/modifying/inspecting users, virtual hosts, exchanges, queues, and bindings
- Backup and recovery of the RabbitMQ database
- Setting up a different database for message persistence
- Taking care of broker security

- Inspecting RabbitMQ logs for errors
- Optimizing resource utilization, tuning performance and monitoring the broker
- Configuring the broker using environment variables, configuration parameters, and policies
- Managing the broker by writing custom applications that make use of the REST API exposed by the RabbitMQ management plugin

Some of the preceding concepts are covered in subsequent chapters. We already saw how easy it is to start/stop/restart instances using the `rabbitmqctl` and `rabbitmq-server` utilities that are part of the standard RabbitMQ installation. Before diving into the nuts and bolts of RabbitMQ administration, let's review the standard directory structure of a typical RabbitMQ server installation. In Windows, run the following command from the installation folder of RabbitMQ:

```
tree /A
```

The following screenshot displays the output from the preceding command:

```
\----rabbitmq_server-3.4.4
    +----db                                         (RabbitMQ database)
    |   +----rabbit@MARTIN-mnesia                    (Mnesia database folder)
    |   |   +----msg_store_persistent                (persistent message store)
    |   |   \----msg_store_transient                 (transient message store)
    |   \----rabbit@MARTIN-plugins-expand            (enabled plugins expand directory)
    +----ebin                                        (Erlang binaries)
    +----etc                                         (RabbitMQ sample configuration)
    +----include                                     (Erlang headers)
    +----log                                         (RabbitMQ log files)
    +----plugins                                     (RabbitMQ plugins)
    \----sbin                                        (RabbitMQ scripts)
```

Mnesia is a distributed NoSQL database used by RabbitMQ to store information about users, vhosts, exchanges, queues, bindings, index files (the position of messages in queues), and cluster information. It can store data either on RAM or on disk. Although persistent messages are stored along with the Mnesia files (in the Mnesia folder), they are not managed by Mnesia. RabbitMQ provides its own persistent storage for messages. On the one hand, persistent messages are stored in the `msg_store_persistent` directory (both when they are persisted when received on a queue or when memory consumption grows beyond a specific threshold); on the other hand, non-persistent (transient) message are persisted in the `msg_store_transient` directory (when memory consumption on a queue grows beyond a specific threshold).

The `ebin` directory contains the Erlang compiled sources. They are cross-platform and are interpreted by the Erlang virtual machine installed on the machine on which the RabbitMQ server is installed.

The `include` directory includes the Erlang header files (similar in notion to C++ header files but for Erlang).

The `log` directory contains the RabbitMQ log files and the Erlang **SASL (System Application Support Libraries)** log files, not to be confused with **SASL (Simple Authentication and Security Layer)**, for which RabbitMQ also provides support, covered in *Chapter 9*, *Security*. Erlang SASL provides support for topics such as error logging, alarm handling, and overload regulation.

The `plugins` directory provides packages for the RabbitMQ binaries.

The `sbin` directory contains the RabbitMQ scripts used for server administration, such as rabbitmq-server.bat and rabbitmqctl.bat under Windows.

The following screenshot illustrates the RabbitMQ folder structure for Ubuntu/Debian:

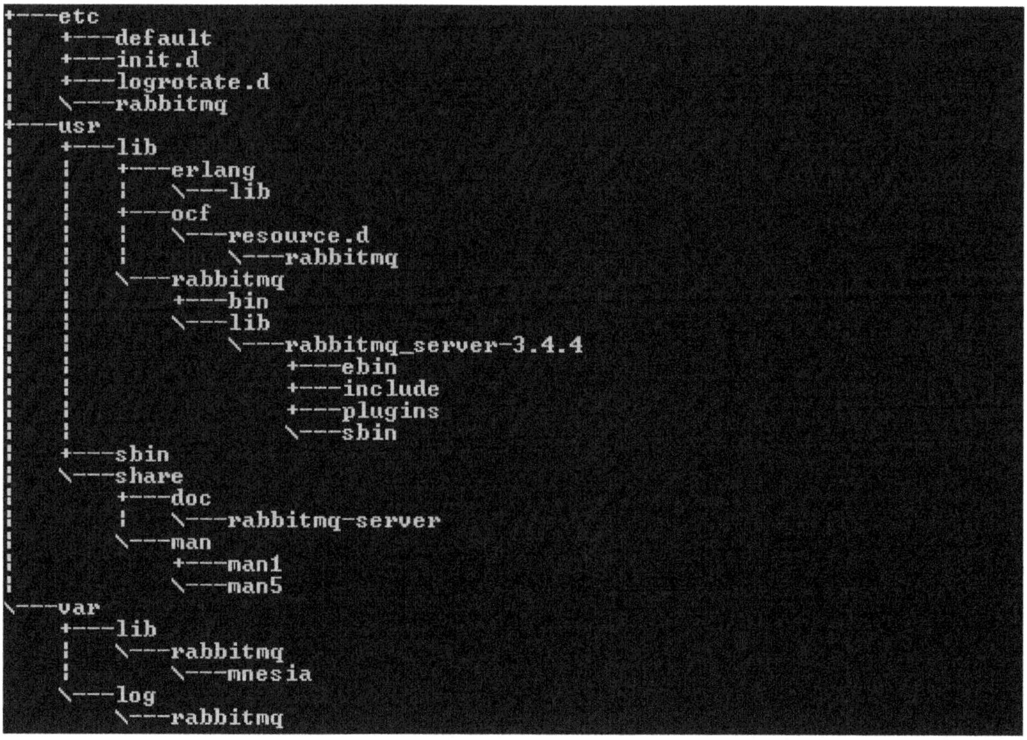

```
+---etc
|   +---default
|   +---init.d
|   +---logrotate.d
|   \---rabbitmq
+---usr
|   +---lib
|   |   +---erlang
|   |   |   \---lib
|   |   +---ocf
|   |   |   \---resource.d
|   |   |       \---rabbitmq
|   |   \---rabbitmq
|   |       +---bin
|   |       \---lib
|   |           \---rabbitmq_server-3.4.4
|   |               +---ebin
|   |               +---include
|   |               +---plugins
|   |               \---sbin
|   +---sbin
|   \---share
|       +---doc
|       |   \---rabbitmq-server
|       \---man
|           +---man1
|           \---man5
\---var
    +---lib
    |   \---rabbitmq
    |       \---mnesia
    \---log
        \---rabbitmq
```

And the following is for a generic Unix installation:

```
+----ebin
+----etc
¦   \----rabbitmq
+----include
+----plugins
+----sbin
\----share
    \----man
        +----man1
        \----man5
```

Note that database and log files are not created until the RabbitMQ broker is started for the first time. If you delete the RabbitMQ database and/or log files, they will be recreated when the broker is started again.

The locations of some parts of the RabbitMQ installation files can be configured using environment variables, such as:

- RABBITMQ_BASE sets the location of the RabbitMQ database and log files. Note that, if it is not set under Windows, then the default location for the variable will be %APPDATA%\RabbitMQ (meaning that your database, log, and configuration files will be stored under that directory unless other configuration parameters are used to change their location). You can set this directory to be the installation folder of your RabbitMQ server if you want to store the database, log, and configuration in the same location as the other RabbitMQ server components.

- RABBITMQ_CONFIG_FILE sets the location of the RabbitMQ configuration file (without the .config extension of the file).

- RABBITMQ_LOG_BASE specifies the base directory for storing RabbitMQ log files.

For more information on the various environment variables related to the directory structure of the RabbitMQ server, you can refer to the RabbitMQ server documentation.

Administering RabbitMQ components

The various RabbitMQ components can be modified in any of the following ways:

- From the web interface of the RabbitMQ management plugin
- From the rabbitmqctl script (in the sbin directory)
- From the REST API of the RabbitMQ management plugin

So far, we have seen how to programmatically create queues, exchanges, and bindings. However, they can be pre-created in the broker so that the overhead of managing them from source code on the producer/consumer side is minimized. Moreover, we can also create users, vhosts, and policies using the management plugin or the rabbitmqctl utility. For some administrative tasks, you can use a command line utility (rabbitmqadmin) that comes with the RabbitMQ management plugin. In order to download it, navigate to `http://localhost:15672/cli/` and save it to a proper location (for example, the `sbin` directory of the RabbitMQ installation; make sure you save it with a `.py` extension since it is a Python script, and ensure you have Python 3 installed before using the script). To view all available commands for the rabbitmqadmin.py script, you can issue the following from the command line:

```
rabbitmqadmin.py help
rabbitmqadmin.py help subcommands
```

Administering users

You can easily create new users from the command line. For example, if you want to create a user with the name `sam` and the password `d1v`, and a user `jim` with the password `tester`, you can issue the following commands:

```
rabbitmqctl add_user sam d1v
rabbitmqctl add_user jim tester
```

The preceding users are regular (non-administrative) users and not assigned to any vhost. At that point, if you try to access the web management console you will receive a login failure. In order to make `sam` an admin user you can issue the following command:

```
rabbitmqctl.bat set_user_tags jim administrator
```

Now `jim` is able to administer the broker and login to the management console. The users still don't have access to any vhost (even the default one). If you navigate to the `Admin` tab in the management console, you will see something like this:

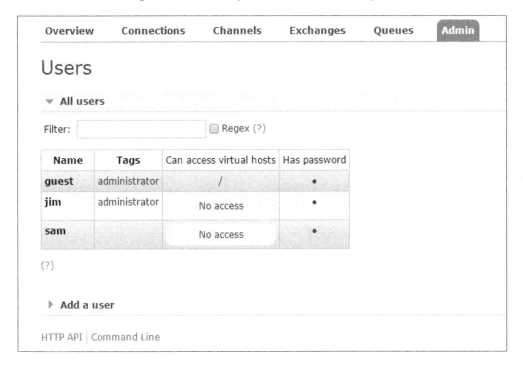

The following command can be used to list all users in the broker instance:

```
rabbitmqctl.bat list_users
```

If you want to change the password for `sam` to `t1ster`, you can issue the following command:

```
rabbitmqctl.bat change_password jim t1ster
```

If you want to delete the user `sam`, you can issue the following command:

```
rabbitmqctl.bat delete_user jim
```

You can also manage users from the RabbitMQ web management interface or the `rabbitmqadmin.py` script. Let's make `sam` an administrator:

```
rabbitmqctl.bat set_user_tags sam administrator
```

Administering vhosts

We have already mentioned that vhosts are used to logically separate a broker instance into multiple domains, each one with its own set of exchanges, queues, and bindings. The following example creates the `chat` and `events` vhost:

```
rabbitmqctl.bat add_vhost chat
rabbitmqctl.bat add_vhost events
```

Note that it might be a better idea to name your vhosts hierarchically (meaning that chat becomes /chat and vhost becomes /vhost; any child vhosts can be added following the same pattern—for example, `/chat/administrators` and `/events/follow`).

If you navigate to the `Admin` tab in the management console and click on Virtual Hosts, you will see something like this:

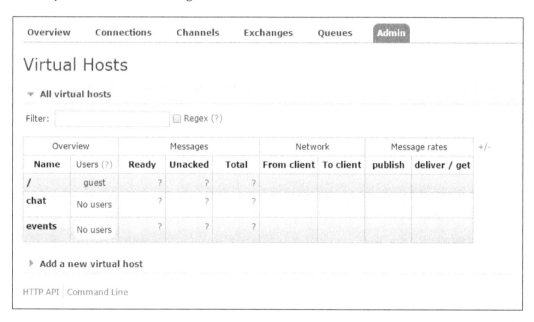

The following command can be used to list all virtual hosts in the broker instance:

```
rabbitmqctl.bat list_vhosts
```

You can use the following command to the delete the `events` vhost:

```
rabbitmqctl.bat delete_vhost events
```

You can also manage vhosts from the RabbitMQ web management interface.

Administering permissions

Now that we have seen how to create users and vhosts, we can assign permissions to particular users so that they are able to access particular vhosts (and all of the RabbitMQ components associated with that vhost). The following example grants configure, write, and read permissions to all resources in the chat vhost to the user jim:

```
rabbitmqctl.bat set_permissions -p chat jim ".*" ".*" ".*"
```

Note that in some cases under Windows, any of the rabbitmqctl commands may not be properly executed due to Erlang issues with encoding under Windows. In that case, you can also use the rabbitmqadmin.py script as follows:

```
rabbitmqadmin.py declare permission vhost=chat user=sam configure=.*
write=.* read=.*
```

As you can see, the configure, write, and read permissions can be regular expressions that match the names of the vhosts components that the user has access to. You can list all permissions in the broker with the following command:

```
rabbitmqctl.bat list_permissions
```

Alternatively, you can use the rabbitmqadmin.py script for this purpose:

```
rabbitmqadmin.py list permissions
```

You can delete the permission given to the user sam for the chat vhost using the following command:

```
rabbitmqctl.bat clear_permissions -p chat sam
```

Alternatively you can use the rabbitmqadmin.py script for this purpose:

```
rabbitmqadmin.py delete permission vhost=chat user=sam
```

If you omit the vhost from the preceding commands, you will clear all permissions assigned to the user sam. You can also list all vhosts to which the user sam is assigned with the following command:

```
rabbitmqadmin -u sam -p d1v list vhosts
```

Administering exchanges

You can create exchanges from the RabbitMQ management web interface or the rabbitmqadmin script. The following example creates the logs fanout exchange in the default vhost:

```
rabbitmqadmin.py declare exchange name=logs type=fanout
```

The following example creates another fanout exchange with the name `logs` in the `chat` vhost (first we set permissions for the guest user to the vhost; otherwise, we have to specify a user that has administrator permissions for the vhost):

```
rabbitmqadmin.py declare permission vhost=chat user=guest
configure=.* write=.* read=.*
rabbitmqadmin.py declare -V chat exchange name=logs type=fanout
```

When declaring an exchange, you can specify additional properties such as exchange durability. To delete the `logs` exchange from the `chat` domain, you can issue:

```
rabbitmqadmin.py -V chat delete exchange name=logs
```

To list all exchanges in the `chat` vhost, you can issue:

```
rabbitmqadmin.py -V chat list exchanges
```

To list all exchanges in the default vhost, you can issue:

```
rabbitmqadmin.py list exchanges
```

Administering queues

You can create queues from the RabbitMQ management web interface or the `rabbitmqadmin` script. The following example creates the non-durable `error_logs` queue in the default vhost:

```
rabbitmqadmin.py declare queue name=error_logs durable=false
```

The following example creates a queue with the same name in the `chat` vhost:

```
rabbitmqadmin.py -V chat declare queue name=error_logs
```

To delete the `error_logs` queue from the `chat` vhost, you can issue the following:

```
rabbitmqadmin.py -V chat delete queue name=error_logs
```

To list all queues in the default domain, you can issue:

```
rabbitmqadmin.py list queues
```

Administering bindings

Now that we have seen how straightforward it is to create exchanges and queues, let's see how to create bindings. The following creates a binding between the `logs` fanout exchange we already created and the `error_logs` queue in the default vhost:

```
rabbitmqadmin.py declare binding source=logs destination=error_logs
```

In order to test that the binding works, we can use the `rabbitmqadmin` script to publish to the `logs` exchange, then read from the `error_logs` queue (here you can check if the message is successfully retrieved from the queue), and finally clear the `error_logs` queue from any messages:

```
rabbitmqadmin.py publish exchange=logs routing_key= payload="new log"
rabbitmqadmin.py get queue=error_logs
rabbitmqadmin.py purge queue name=error_logs
```

Administering policies

Policies allow you to define (and change) certain properties of exchanges and queues at runtime. Since no more than one policy can be defined per exchange/queue, a policy can incorporate multiple settings at once. Let's consider the following scenarios:

- We decide to set a limit on the capacity of a queue; if it is exceeded then the messages are either dropped or dead-lettered (meaning they are redirected to an alternative exchange)

- We decide to set a limit on the time that a message is allowed to stay in a queue; if that time is exceeded for a message then it is either dropped or dead-lettered

- We want to define a dead-letter exchange that receives dead-letter messages from one or more queues

In order to set the capacity of the `error_logs` queue in the default ('/') vhost to 200,000 bytes, you can apply the following policy:

```
rabbitmqctl  set_policy max-queue-len "error_logs" "{""max-length-
bytes"" : 200000}" apply-to queue
```

You can also use the rabbitmqadmin.py script for this purpose:

```
rabbitmqadmin.py declare policy name=max-queue-len pattern=error_logs
definition="{""max-length-bytes"":200000}" apply-to=queues
```

The following policy sets the maximum queue length in terms of messages (if you want to apply it you must first drop the previously created policy):

```
rabbitmqadmin.py declare policy name=max-queue-len pattern=error_logs
definition="{""max-length"":200000}" apply-to=queues
```

Notice that instead of the name of the queue (`error_logs` in that case), you can specify a pattern for the names of the queues to which the policy applies. This means that policies apply to queues that match the pattern and they are added after the policy is created. To delete the policy you can issue:

```
rabbitmqctl.bat clear_policy max-queue-len
```

Alternatively you can issue:

```
rabbitmqadmin.py delete policy name=max-queue-len
```

Note that the queue length might also be set from the client using the `x-max-length` arguments passed to the arguments map in the declaration of a queue from the client.

In order to set the **TTL (time-to-live)** of the messages to all queues in the default vhost to three seconds, you can apply the following policy:

```
rabbitmqadmin.py declare policy name=ttl pattern=.*
definition="{""message-ttl"":3000}" apply-to=queues
```

Note that the message TTL for the queue might also be set from the client using the `x-message-ttl` arguments passed to the arguments map in the declaration of a queue from the client or on a per-message basis using the `expiration` field set properly on the `AMQP.BasicProperties` instance passed when publishing a message. You can also set expiration for the entire queue, which means that the queue will be automatically deleted after a certain period of idle time; this is particularly useful when a large number of queues is created and they need to be purged over time. The following example sets the queue TTL for all queues starting with the `response` prefix to 10 minutes:

```
rabbitmqadmin.py declare policy name=queue-ttl
pattern=response.* definition="{""expires"":600000}" apply-to=queues
```

Note that the queue TTL might also be set from the client using the `x-queue` arguments passed to the arguments map in the declaration of a queue from the client.

If a message TTL expires, the queue capacity is exhausted, or a message received from a queue is explicitly rejected from a consumer, it can be routed to an alternative dead-letter exchange. The following diagram provides an overview of the scenario:

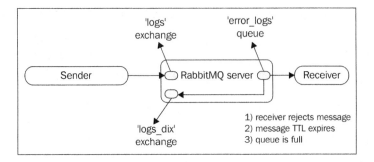

The following example creates the `logs_dlx` exchange and sets it as a dead-letter exchange to the `error_logs` queue:

```
rabbitmqadmin.py declare exchange name=logs_dlx type=fanout
rabbitmqadmin.py declare policy name=ttl
pattern="^error_logs$" definition="{""dead-letter-exchange"": ""logs_
dlx"", ""message-ttl"":3000}" apply-to=queues
```

Note that if we use only `"error_logs"` instead of `"^error_logs$"` then `error_logs_dlx` will also be matched and we don't want this to happen. Notice that in the preceding example we combined the dead-letter-exchange policy with the message-ttl policy. You can list all policies with the following command:

```
rabbitmqadmin.py list policies
```

Note that you have to make sure that only one policy applies at a time on a queue; if two or more patterns match a queue name then it becomes unclear which policy will be applied. If that happens, remove policies that apply to a queue and combine them in a single composite policy. To delete the `max-queue-len` policy we created earlier, issue the following command:

```
rabbitmqadmin.py delete policy name=max-queue-len
```

In order to test that the dead-letter exchange is properly configured we can use the following scenario:

- Create a queue named `error_logs_dlx` that binds to the `logs_dlx` exchange
- Send a message to the `logs` exchange

- Wait for more than three seconds
- Check that the message can be consumed from `error_logs_dlx`
- Clear the `error_logs_dlx` queue

The following example can be used to test the preceding scenario:

```
rabbitmqadmin.py declare queue name=error_logs_dlx
rabbitmqadmin.py declare binding source=logs_dlx
destination=error_logs_dlx
rabbitmqadmin.py publish exchange=logs routing_key=      payload="dlx
message"
```

Wait at least three seconds and execute the following in order to verify that the message is sent to the dead-letter queue (clearing the queue at the end):

```
rabbitmqadmin.py get queue=error_logs_dlx
rabbitmqadmin.py purge queue name=error_logs
```

Administering the RabbitMQ database

The RabbitMQ database stores both message server metadata and messages from queues. In the next sections we will see how can we manage this database for the purpose of disaster recovery.

Full backup and restore

As we have already seen, RabbitMQ uses Mnesia to store information about the various components of the broker as well as cluster configuration and a custom database for storing persistent messages. In that regard it is straightforward to back up the contents of the RabbitMQ database:

- Stop the broker
- Copy the Mnesia folder and archive it
- Restart the broker

The restore procedure, as you might have guessed, is pretty similar. You should also consider the fact that if a message is not persistent it may not be backed up using the preceding procedure since it is not written to the persistent store of RabbitMQ (in the event of a crash). In order for a message to be persistent, the exchange and queue through which it passes must be durable (marked as such during creation) and the message must be marked as persistent (with a delivery mode set to 2 from the sender). A response for a successfully received persistent message is not sent until a message is written to the persistent log file on an exchange. You may be wondering about the case when a live backup must be made on the RabbitMQ database with preservation of messages at a particular point in time. In this case you have a number of options to consider, such as:

- Using the exchange-to-exchange bindings extension that allows you to pass a message through multiple exchanges. In this regard you can create a separate exchange for backup purposes and bind all other exchanges to that one; a dedicated queue bound to that exchange can be used to save messages to a persistent store along with a timestamp for a custom point-in time recovery implementation.

- Creating a federated exchange (in the same or another broker), linked to all exchanges in the broker, that receives all of the messages published to exchanges from the broker. The federated exchange can then be bound to a dedicated queue that can be used to save messages to a persistent store along with a timestamp for a custom point-in time recovery implementation; the Federation plugin is required for that purpose.

- Replicating messages from all queues to a destination exchange using shovels; the Shovel plugin is required for that purpose.

In many cases however you may need to backup/restore only the configuration of RabbitMQ components at a particular point in time.

Backing up and restoring the broker metadata

In order to back up the RabbitMQ broker metadata (the configuration of broker components) you can use the rabbitmqadmin management plugin as follows (assuming we want to backup the broker configuration to a file named broker.export in the current directory):

```
rabbitmqadmin.py export broker.json
```

If you open the file you will notice that there is a section for each type of component, along with the version of the broker:

```
{
    "rabbit_version":"3.4.4",
    "users":[
        {
            "name":"sam",
            "password_hash":"y7CFOccmv5tReRwEskXapNOSsmM=",
            "tags":"administrator"
        },
        ….
    ],
    "vhosts":[
        {
            "name":"chat"
        },
        {
            "name":"/"
        }
    ],
    ...
}
```

To import back the configuration, you can use the following command:

```
rabbitmqadmin.py import broker.json
```

Note that it is a good idea to add a user-readable timestamp to the name of the export file, based on the utilities provided by your OS for that purpose. You can also perform the export/import of the current RabbitMQ configuration for the management web interface from the **Overview** tab.

Installing RabbitMQ plugins

So far, we have used the rabbitmq-plugins utility in order to enable the management plugin (already part of the RabbitMQ installation). You may want to install additional (for example, community) plugins that allow you to extend the features of the broker, thus giving you the opportunity to implement a wider range of messaging scenarios. Installing a plugin is a two-step process:

- Download the ez archive (Erlang ZIP archive) of the plugin and copy it to the `plugins` folder from the RabbitMQ installation
- Enable the plugin with the rabbitmq-plugins utility

Let's say we want to be able to send e-mails from our messages directly from the RabbitMQ instance that receives the messages. For that reason, you can install the rabbitmq_email plugin that provides the AMQP-SMTP and SMTP-AMQP protocol conversion plugins. Download the AMQP-SMTP plugin from `https://www.` `rabbitmq.com/community-plugins/v3.4.x/gen_smtp-0.9.0-rmq3.4.x-61e19ec5-` `gita62c02e.ez` and copy it to the `plugins` folder in the RabbitMQ installation. You can see that the plugin can now be managed from the broker by issuing:

```
rabbitmq-plugins.bat list
```

You should see that the `gen_smtp` plugin is present in the lists and points to the archive we copied to the `plugins` folder. In order to enable it, you can issue the following:

```
rabbitmq-plugins.bat enable gen_smtp
```

To delete a plugin you can disable it and remove it from the `plugins` directory.

Configuring RabbitMQ instances

RabbitMQ configuration can be established in several ways:

- By setting proper environment variables
- By modifying the RabbitMQ configuration file
- By defining runtime parameters and policies that can be modified at runtime

Setting environment variables

Environment variables can be set using a standard mechanism provided by your OS (for example, using the Control Panel in Windows or setting them permanently from the shell in Linux). However they can also be specified in the scripts used to run the RabbitMQ broker, such as the `rabbitmq-server` utility, the `rabbitmq-service` utility (used in Windows to start RabbitMQ as a Windows service), or `rabbitmq-env.conf` (using in Unix-like operating systems by RabbitMQ to configure environment variables). At the beginning of the chapter we covered several such variables related to the location of the RabbitMQ database, logs, and configuration file. Here are several more you can configure:

- `RABBITMQ_NODE_IP_ADDRESS`: The IP address of network interface to which you want to bind the RabbitMQ broker. This is useful if you have multiple such interfaces on the machine where the broker is installed and you want to bind it to only one of them (an empty value means that the broker is bound to all network interface addresses).

- `RABBITMQ_NODE_PORT`: The port on which the RabbitMQ broker listens.

- `RABBITMQ_NODENAME`: The name of the RabbitMQ broker instance (this is required in a clustered configuration—more on that in the next chapter).

- `RABBITMQ_SERVICENAME`: The name of the Windows service for the RabbitMQ broker instance.

Modifying the RabbitMQ configuration file

The rabbitmq configuration file (`rabbitqm.config`) can be used to provide additional configuration of the broker, such as how much RAM the broker is allowed to consume before messages are flushed to the hard disk (`vm_memory_high_watermark`); what IP addresses and ports of the network interfaces the broker listens on (`tcp_listeners`); or what the maximum file size is of the RabbitMQ message stores— both transient and persistent (`msg_store_file_size_limit`). If that limit is exceeded then messages are garbage-collected. The default location for `rabbitmq.config` is under the `%RABBITMQ_BASE%` directory; if RabbitMQ is not specified under Windows the default location of the file will be under `%APPDATA%`. There is a sample configuration file in the etc directory for the installation of the RabbitMQ server. If you copy it and save it under the root installation directory of RabbitMQ with the name `rabbitmq.config`, you can simply uncomment and change the various configuration parameters based on your preferences. Here is a sample configuration that sets limits on the used RAM and message store size:

```
[
  {rabbit,
    [
    {vm_memory_high_watermark, 0.4},
    {msg_store_file_size_limit, 16777216}
    ]
  }
]
```

Managing RabbitMQ instances

RabbitMQ provides a number of utilities for managing RabbitMQ instances since the AMQP protocol provides limited support for that purpose (and it is not a responsibility of the protocol in general to do so). So far we have seen how we can administer RabbitMQ from the command line using the rabbitmqctl or the rabbitmqadmin utilities. However there are many scenarios where more sophisticated tools for provisioning and managing the RabbitMQ broker components are needed (for example, in the form of an alternative web interface).

In that case, the management plugin provides an interface of REST (Representational State Transfer)-based web services. In order to see all the available services in your current installation of the management plugin you can navigate from the browser to `http://localhost:15672/api/`—there is a short description with basic examples and a reference guide for the various services. For testing purposes, you can use any utility (such as cURL) that allows you to send HTTP requests to the manage REST API. As everything in REST is a resource that is managed with CRUD operations provided by the HTTP methods (such as GET, POST, PUT, DELETE), so are RabbitMQ resources. If you take a closer look you will notice that all of the resources are precisely the various types of RabbitMQ components (such as vhosts, users, permissions, queues, exchanges, and bindings); no rocket science here. The REST interface respects the current user permissions (configure, write, read for particular components) when checking for permissions for performing a certain action.

Let's assume that we want to implement a simple utility called ComponentFinder that allows us to list particular RabbitMQ components in a given vhost based on a regular expression. For that purpose we will create a new Maven project that uses the REST client from the Apache Jersey library provided as a Maven dependency, along with the standard JSON utility in Java:

```
<dependency>
    <groupId>com.sun.jersey</groupId>
    <artifactId>jersey-client</artifactId>
    <version>1.19</version>
</dependency>
<dependency>
    <groupId>org.json</groupId>
    <artifactId>json</artifactId>
    <version>20140107</version>
</dependency>
```

Here is the class for the ComponentFinder utility:

```
import java.util.Scanner;
import java.util.regex.Pattern;

import org.json.JSONArray;
import org.json.JSONObject;
import org.slf4j.Logger;
import org.slf4j.LoggerFactory;

import com.sun.jersey.api.client.Client;
import com.sun.jersey.api.client.WebResource;
```

```
import com.sun.jersey.api.client.filter.HTTPBasicAuthFilter;

public class ComponentFinder {

    private final static Logger LOGGER = LoggerFactory
        .getLogger(ComponentFinder.class);
private static final String API_ROOT =
"http://localhost:15672/api";
```

The `main()` method provides the logic for the tool, reading from the standard input and processing the request based on the input parameters. A simple HTTP client is used for the purpose:

```
    public static void main(String[] args) {

        Scanner scanner = null;
        try {
            scanner = new Scanner(System.in);
            System.out.println("Enter component type in
plural form (for example, queues, exchanges) ");
            String type = scanner.nextLine();
            System.out.println("Enter vhost (leave empty
for default vhost) ");
            String vhost = scanner.nextLine();
            System.out.println("Enter name pattern (leave
empty for match-all pattern)");
            String pattern = scanner.nextLine();

            Client client = Client.create();
            String path;
            if (vhost.trim().isEmpty()) {
                path = API_ROOT + "/" + type +
"?columns=name";
            } else {
                path = API_ROOT + "/" + type +
"/" + vhost + "?columns=name";
            }

            WebResource resource = client.resource(path);
            resource.header("Content-Type",
"application/json;charset=UTF-8");
            resource.addFilter(new HTTPBasicAuthFilter("guest",
"guest".getBytes()));
            String result = resource.get(String.class);
```

```
                JSONArray jsonResult = new JSONArray(result);
                LOGGER.debug("Result: \n" + jsonResult.toString(4));
    filterResult(jsonResult, pattern);
        } finally {
            if (scanner != null) {
                scanner.close();
            }
        }
    }
```

The `filterResult()` helper method is used to filter the response from the management API based on a regular expression:

```
private static void filterResult(JSONArray jsonResult,
String pattern) {
        // filter the result based on the pattern
        for (int index = 0; index < jsonResult.length();
index++) {
            JSONObject componentInfo =
(JSONObject) jsonResult.get(index);
            String componentName =
(String) componentInfo.get("name");
            if (Pattern.matches(pattern, componentName)) {
                LOGGER.info("Matched component: " +
componentName);
                // do something else with component
            }
        }
    }}
```

Upgrading RabbitMQ

Upgrading RabbitMQ can be considered in two directions:

- Upgrading the Erlang installation
- Upgrading the broker installation

In both cases, it is good practice to perform a full backup of the RabbitMQ broker before performing an upgrade. Also you should check out the release notes for all the versions issued between the old and the new version to see if there are any specific steps that must be performed during the update. Typically, installation of a RabbitMQ broker preserves data and updates only the RabbitMQ installation and the database structures used for representing the broker metadata and message stores. It is important to make sure that, if you have to update nodes in a cluster, you first stop all nodes and use the same version of RabbitMQ for the update over all nodes in the cluster.

Case study: Administering CSN

For easier management, we have decided to pre-configure our CSN RabbitMQ broker (using a custom script) with two separate vhosts:

- v_chat: For handling all chat messages in CSN
- v_events: For handling of all events in CSN

Moreover we have decided to separate the users that are allowed to access each vhost. The users of the v_events group are further divided into the following logical groups:

- Administrators have the ability to create event queues, and publish and consume messages
- event_publishers have the ability to publish messages
- event_subscribers have the ability to consume messages

As you may guess, we can implement the preceding logical separation easily for the users in the v_events host using policies. The users of the v_chat vhosts have full configure, read, and write access to the components of the vhost.

Another thing we want to provide is the ability to log all messages that pass through the broker for backup and restore purposes. We also decide to set limitations on the RAM and disk storage used by the broker using a custom `rabbitmq.config` file.

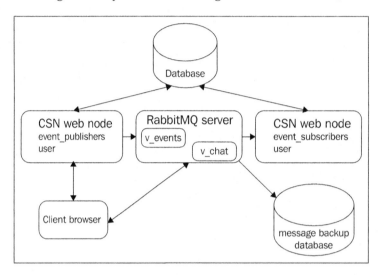

You can provision the additional components as part of the setup process easily by using custom code and the REST API, which allows to create the vhosts, users for them (with the appropriate policies to act as access control based on the logical separation of the users), and a backup exchange that receives a copy of all messages passed to all other exchanges in the broker. A custom utility (that could be part of the backup databases as well) subscribes to that exchange and stores the messages in the database.

Summary

In this chapter, we saw how to administer a standalone RabbitMQ broker along with its components, users, vhosts, permissions, queues, exchanges, bindings, and policies. We discussed the structure of a typical RabbitMQ installation (along with the parameters that allow us to configure different locations for various parts of the broker) and how to provide further configuration in terms of environment variables and the `rabbitmq.config` file. We discussed administrative tasks such as backing up and restoring the RabbitMQ database, updating a RabbitMQ broker, and plugin installation and management of the broker using the management REST API. In the next chapter we will explore what clustering support the message broker provides for the purpose of scalability.

Exercises

1. What utilities can you use to create users, vhosts, and policies in a RabbitMQ broker?

2. What utilities can you use to create exchanges, queues, and bindings?

3. How can you back up and restore RabbitMQ broker metadata?

4. How can you set limits on the maximum RAM and disk space for storing messages in RabbitMQ?

5. What happens when the various resource limits set on the broker are exceeded?

6. Assuming you need to migrate the RabbitMQ message stores to a larger disk mounted on the current machine, how can you do it?

7. A new version of RabbitMQ comes out that provides a major security fix. How can you upgrade your installation of RabbitMQ?

4
Clustering

So far, we have been dealing with a single RabbitMQ instance, thus demonstrating the various capabilities of the message broker. However RabbitMQ provides a built-in clustering mechanism that can be used in a variety of scenarios related to large scale production deployments of RabbitMQ.

Topics covered in the chapter:

- Benefits of clustering
- Clustering support in RabbitMQ
- A case study on scaling the CSN

Benefits of clustering

So far we have discussed how to use a single RabbitMQ instance for handling various types of message. However, in many production scenarios the number of messages that needs to be processed may increase rapidly over time that this should not impact the time required to process a single message – now we have a problem. To resolve it we need to be able to scale our RabbitMQ server deployment. RabbitMQ clustering support provides a mechanism for horizontally scaling RabbitMQ instances. This essentially means that multiple RabbitMQs can be configured to work as a single logical unit in the form of a clustered message broker.

This provides the means to distribute workloads among instances in a cluster, link clients to different instances in a cluster (thus distributing the number of clients linked to a single instance), or even establish high availability of the messaging broker:

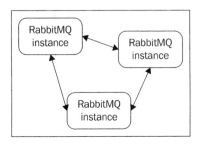

RabbitMQ clustering support

RabbitMQ clustering is based on the underlying Erlang message-passing interface. Messages between Erlang processes are just Erlang terms which can be processed by the receiving instance. Communication between the nodes is established by means of the so called magic cookie (or Erlang cookie), which provides a mechanism to authenticate nodes in a cluster with each other. Once a new node is started, its cookie (the .erlang.cookie file) is read from the home directory of the user (denoted by the $HOME environment variable in Uni-based operating systems or by the %HOMEPATH% variable in Windows-based operating systems). If the cookie does not exist then it is created based on information from the current node. Once retrieved, the cookie is set for the Erlang process with erlang:set_cookie(node(), Cookie). Later, when we try to connect the node to a RabbitMQ cluster, we retrieve the cookie with erlang:get_cookie() and compare it against the cookies of the other nodes in the cluster – if they don't match, the connection of the node to the cluster is rejected.

All nodes in the cluster see information about the elements of a cluster such as virtual hosts, users, permissions, exchanges, bindings, and queues. When you add new nodes to the cluster they only receive the cluster metadata and not the contents of the queues in the cluster, which not only saves you disk space but also improves performance since messages are not replicated by default across the cluster nodes (although they can be replicated across RabbitMQ instances for high-availability, as we shall see in a separate chapter).

In order to be able to establish a RabbitMQ cluster, the following prerequisites must be met:

- All of the machines where RabbitMQ instances reside must have the same version of RabbitMQ and Erlang installed
- All of the instances must have the same Erlang cookie (since Erlang message passing is used to establish communication between the brokers)

Creating a simple cluster

Let's create a simple RabbitMQ cluster with three nodes on the local machine. The steps we can follow in order to do this are:

- Disable all plug-ins before starting the node instances – this is required in order to avoid problems with plug-ins such as the management-plugin, which already runs on port 15672 – if you don't disable it and it is already running as part of the another RabbitMQ instance on the same machine, then attempting to start a node will fail since the node will try to start the management plug-in on the same port unless you provide a different configuration with a different management port for the particular plug-in.
- You don't have to worry about this since the RabbitMQ management plug-in is aware of clusters and it is sufficient to start the plug-in only for one of the instances in the cluster. If you want to enable a failover configuration for the management plug-in you can start it for two or more nodes running on different ports.
- Start three independent RabbitMQ node instances on the current machine.
- Add nodes to the cluster by specifying at least one active node in the cluster for the purpose. You can specify more than one active node in the cluster but at least one is needed to join the node to all the other nodes currently in the cluster.

The first step can be accomplished by executing the following command:

```
rabbitmq-plugins.bat disable rabbitmq_management
```

The second step is also pretty straightforward. The root node in the cluster is already present – that is the instance of RabbitMQ that we were running so far. You just need to execute the following commands in order to the start two more independent nodes (named `instance2` and `instance3` and running on different ports):

```
set RABBITMQ_NODENAME=instance1 &
set RABBITMQ_NODE_PORT=5701 &
rabbitmq-server.bat –detached
```

```
set RABBITMQ_NODENAME=instance2 &
set RABBITMQ_NODE_PORT=5702 &
rabbitmq-server.bat -detached
```

If you are using a Unix-based operating system, the preceding commands will look like the following:

```
RABBITMQ_NODENAME=instance1 &&
RABBITMQ_NODE_PORT=5701 &&
./rabbitmq-server.sh -detached

RABBITMQ_NODENAME=instance2 &&
RABBITMQ_NODE_PORT=5702 &&
./rabbitmq-server.bat -detached
```

If you are using the default installation on Windows then a standalone instance will already be running with some specified name (upon installation of the broker) and using the default node port of 5672 and distribution port of 25672 (the 20000 + node port value). That is why we need to specify different names and distribution ports when starting the instances.

Adding nodes to the cluster

Now let's add the two nodes we created and started to the cluster – currently consisting only of a single node. To verify this, you can run the following command:

```
rabbitmqctl.bat cluster_status
```

You will see something like this in the output:

```
[s
{nodes,
    [{disc, [rabbit@DOMAIN]}]},
{running_nodes,[rabbit@DOMAIN]},
{cluster_name,<<»rabbit@Domain»>>},
{partitions,[]}
]
```

The cluster configuration lists the current nodes in the cluster – these could be either DISK or RAM nodes. By default, nodes are created as DISK nodes, meaning that they persist cluster metadata on disk. RAM nodes allow for optimizations among the cluster nodes since they store everything in memory rather than persisting information on disk. This trade-off between loss of data and performance depends on the particular messaging requirements of the application. In the preceding example, we can see that there is only one DISK node currently running and that the name of the cluster is inherited from the name of the root node.

Let's add the `instance1` node to the cluster:

```
rabbitmqctl.bat -ninstance1 stop_app
rabbitmqctl.bat -n instance1 join_cluster rabbit@DOMAIN
rabbitmqctl.bat -n instance1 start_app
```

In case `instance1` was not a new instance and already had some metadata such as queues, exchanges, or vhosts, then after the `app_stop` step you have to clear the state of the node as follows before joining it to the cluster:

```
rabbitmqctl.bat -n instance1 reset
```

If the preceding commands succeed, you should get the following sequence of messages:

```
Stopping node instance1@Domain ...
Clustering node instance1@Domain with rabbit@DOMAIN ...
Starting node instance1@Domain ...
```

Now let's also add the second node to the cluster:

```
rabbitmqctl.bat -n instance2 stop_app
rabbitmqctl.bat -n instance2 join_cluster rabbit@DOMAIN
rabbitmqctl.bat -n instance2 start_app
```

Note that you have to provide only a single node in the cluster rather than a list of all nodes – RabbitMQ automatically clusters the node with all other nodes existing in the cluster . We simply specify just one of them (the only condition is that the node must be up-and-running).

If we check again the configuration of the cluster again:

```
rabbitmqctl.bat cluster_status
```

We will see something like this:

```
[
{nodes,
    [{disc,[instance1@DOMAIN, instance2@DOMAIN, rabbit@DOMAIN]}]},
{running_nodes,[instance1@DOMAIN, instance2@DOMAIN, rabbit@DOMAIN]},
{cluster_name,<<»rabbit@Domain»>>},
{partitions,[]}
]
```

Since the management console is already enabled for the root node in the cluster (`rabbit@DOMAIN`), if we go the **Overview** tab we will see the three nodes under the **Nodes** section:

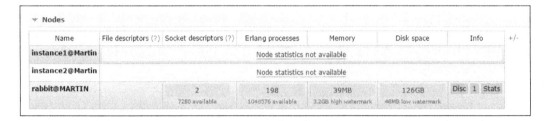

At that point we have a fully functional RabbitMQ cluster with three DISC nodes. Let's see how to add RAM nodes to our cluster.

If you notice, there are some statistics displayed for the root node such as used/available Erlang processes, used/available memory, and a few others. However, for the other two nodes we added to the cluster a **Node statistics not available** message is being displayed. This is due to the fact that we have disabled the management plug-in for the two nodes before starting them and it requires the `rabbitmq_management_agent` plug-in that is required in order to display statistics for the instances from the RabbitMQ management plug-in running over a cluster node. The following enables the management agent plug-in on the instances:

```
rabbitmq-plugins.bat -n instance1 enable rabbitmq_management_agent
rabbitmq-plugins.bat -n instance2 enable rabbitmq_management_agent
```

If we now go to the **Overview** tab, we will see that statistics are displayed for all three nodes:

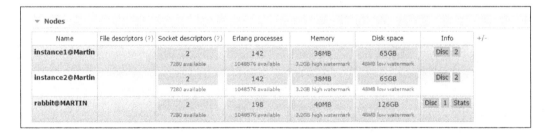

We can also configure the RabbitMQ cluster nodes directly in the RabbitMQ configuration—we just specify a list of running RabbitMQ instances as identified by their name—and once the node starts up it will try to cluster against the list of nodes. There are some prerequisites when RabbitMQ tries to create the cluster from the configuration—the nodes must be in a clean state, the same version of RabbitMQ must be running over them, and they must have the same Erlang cookie. To make sure that the nodes are in a clean state (if they are not newly created), reset their state with the `rabbitmqctl` utility:

```
rabbitmqctl.bat -n instance1 reset
```

To make sure they are running the same version of RabbitMQ you can use the `rabbitmqctl` utility again:

```
rabbitmqctl.bat -n instance1 status
```

Note that, in our case, the preceding code is not relevant since we are running the instances from the same installation of RabbitMQ. If the instances were running on different versions of the broker (on the same or different machines), then we could upgrade all of the nodes with the same version of RabbitMQ. In order to perform the upgrade, however, we must designate one of the DISK nodes as the upgrader node that will synchronize the cluster nodes once the upgrade is done – that node should be stopped last and started first when the entire cluster is brought down to upgrade the nodes. To make sure the nodes have the same cookie, just copy it over to all the nodes from the root node in the cluster.

Another consideration is that nodes might be running behind firewalls and in that case you have to make sure that the ports used by RabbitMQ are opened–one is 4369 (unless changed) and is used by the `epmd` port mapper process that is used to resolve host names in the cluster. The other port is the distribution port for the node – for `instance1` in our case that is 5701 and for `instance2` 5702 (these are the ports we assigned to the nodes when starting them).

Adding RAM-only nodes to the cluster

Adding a RAM only node to our cluster is similar to how we add a DISK node but with one additional parameter. The following example adds the `instance3` RAM node to the cluster:

```
set RABBITMQ_NODENAME=instance3 &
set RABBITMQ_NODE_PORT=5703 &
rabbitmq-server.bat –detached
rabbitmqctl.bat -n instance3 stop_app
rabbitmqctl.bat -n instance3 join_cluster --ram rabbit@DOMAIN
rabbitmqctl.bat -n instance3 start_app
```

If we now check the cluster status:

```
rabbitmqctl.bat cluster_status
```

We will see that the `instance3` node is registered as a RAM node to the cluster:

```
[
{nodes,
    [{disc, [instance1@DOMAIN, instance2@DOMAIN, rabbit@DOMAIN],
      {ram, [instance3@Domain] }
      ]},
   {running_nodes, [ instance3@Domain, instance1@DOMAIN, instance2@
DOMAIN,                 rabbit@DOMAIN] },
   {cluster_name,<<»rabbit@Domain»>>},
   {partitions, []}
]
```

You can also switch the node to DISK mode using the `rabbitmqctl` utility – you must first stop the running RabbitMQ application on the node:

```
rabbitmqctl.bat -n instance3 change_cluster_node_type disk
```

Removing nodes from a cluster

Let's assume that we want to remove the `instance2` node from the cluster. First we have to stop the RabbitMQ application on that node and leave only the Erlang process running:

```
rabbitmqctl.bat -n instance2 stop_app
```

At that point `instance2` is still registered to the cluster but is not running (this can be verified from the status of the cluster). Now you have to remove the node itself from the cluster. This can be done by resetting the node or directly removing the node from the cluster first and later resetting it. Even if you remove the node from the cluster without resetting it, the node configuration still implies that it is part of a cluster and it still needs to be reset. To first remove the `instance2` node from the cluster, you can execute the following command:

```
rabbitmqctl.bat forget_cluster_node instance2@Domain
```

At that point the `instance2` node is removed from the cluster. You also have to reset its state:

```
rabbitmqctl.bat -n instance2 reset
```

Connecting to the cluster

Now let's see how to connect to the cluster we created and experiment with it. Let's assume that we have a publisher sending messages on one instance of the cluster and a subscriber on another instance of the cluster, as outlined in the following diagram:

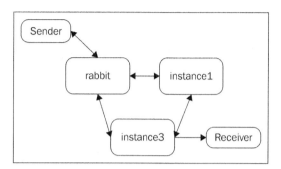

The `ClusterSender` class provides the implementation of a message sender that uses the default exchange in order to publish to the `event_queue` queue – it is a modified variant of the `Sender` class we used when we discussed messaging patterns with RabbitMQ – refer to *Chapter 2, Design Patterns with RabbitMQ*, for details of the implementation. There is one core difference – the `initialize()` method accepts a list of addresses (hostname/port pairs) that represent the instance to which the sender connects upon initialization:

```
public class ClusterSender {
    private final stsatic Logger LOGGER =
LoggerFactory.getLogger(Sender.class);
    private final static String QUEUE_NAME = "event_queue";
    private static final String DEFAULT_EXCHANGE = "";

    private Channel channel;
    private Connection connection;

    public void initialize(Address... hosts) {
        try {

            ConnectionFactory factory =
    new ConnectionFactory();
            factory.setHost("localhost");
            connection = factory.newConnection(hosts);
            channel = connection.createChannel();
        } catch (IOException e) {
```

```
                LOGGER.error(e.getMessage(), e);
            }
        }

    public void send(String message) {
        try {
            channel.queueDeclare(QUEUE_NAME,
false, false, false, null);
            channel.basicPublish(DEFAULT_EXCHANGE,
 QUEUE_NAME, null, message.getBytes());
        } catch (IOException e) {
            LOGGER.error(e.getMessage(), e);
        }
    }

    public void destroy() {
        try {
            if (connection != null) {
                connection.close();
            }
        } catch (IOException e) {
            LOGGER.warn(e.getMessage(), e);
        }
    }
}
```

The ClusterReceiver class provides the implementation of a receiver that retrieves a single message from the event_queue queue. It also extends the variant of a receiver we already introduced earlier and the initialize() method is also extended to accept a list of addresses that represent one or more nodes in the cluster we would like to connect to:

```
public class ClusterReceiver {

    private final static String QUEUE_NAME = "event_queue";
    private final static Logger LOGGER =                 LoggerFactory.
getLogger(ClusterReceiver.class);

    private Connection connection = null;
    private Channel channel = null;

    public void initialize(Address ...hosts) {
        try {
            ConnectionFactory factory =                 new
ConnectionFactory();
```

```
            factory.setHost("localhost");
            connection = factory.newConnection(hosts);
            channel = connection.createChannel();
        } catch (IOException e) {
            LOGGER.error(e.getMessage(), e);
        }
    }

    public String receive(Address ...hosts) {

        if (channel == null) {
            initialize(hosts);
        }

        String message = null;
        try {
            channel.queueDeclare(QUEUE_NAME,
false, false, false, null);
            QueueingConsumer consumer =                    new
QueueingConsumer(channel);
            channel.basicConsume(QUEUE_NAME, true, consumer);

            QueueingConsumer.Delivery delivery =
consumer.nextDelivery();
            message = new String(delivery.getBody());
            LOGGER.info("Message received: " + message);
            return message;

        } catch (IOException e) {
            LOGGER.error(e.getMessage(), e);
        } catch (ShutdownSignalException e) {
            LOGGER.error(e.getMessage(), e);
        } catch (ConsumerCancelledException e) {
            LOGGER.error(e.getMessage(), e);
        } catch (InterruptedException e) {
            LOGGER.error(e.getMessage(), e);
        }

        return message;
    }

    public void destroy() {
        if (connection != null) {
            try {
```

```
                connection.close();
            } catch (IOException e) {
                LOGGER.warn(e.getMessage(), e);
            }
        }
    }
}
```

Let's first subscribe the receiver to the `instance3` node by running the `main()` method of the `ClusterSenderDemo` class:

```
public class ClusterReceiverDemo {

    private static final String NODE_HOSTNAME = "localhost";

    // this is the port on which instance3 is running
    private static final int NODE_PORT = 5703;

    public static void main(String[] args) throws
InterruptedException {
        final ClusterReceiver receiver = new ClusterReceiver();
        receiver.initialize(new Address(NODE_HOSTNAME, NODE_PORT));
        receiver.receive();
        receiver.destroy();
    }
}
```

After you have subscribed to the cluster (on the `instance3` node) run the `main()` method of the `ClusterSenderDemo` class in order to send a message on the default exchange (on the `rabbit` node):

```
public class ClusterSenderDemo {

    private static final String NODE_HOSTNAME = "localhost";

    // default port 5672 which corresponds
    // to the 'rabbit@Domain' instance
    // is being used for the connection to the broker
    public static void sendToDefaultExchange() {
        ClusterSender sender = new ClusterSender();
        Address address = new Address(NODE_HOSTNAME);
        sender.initialize(address);
```

```
        sender.send("Test message.");

        sender.destroy();
    }

    public static void main(String[] args) {
        sendToDefaultExchange();
    }
}
```

You will notice that the receiver received the message successfully:

```
INFO   ClusterReceiver:51 - Message received: Test message.
```

In order to understand what exactly happened, it is essential to understand that it is actually the connection channel that routes the message; the default exchange is just a logical name used to indicate to the channel where to route the message. In that regard the channel that connected the sender to the `rabbit` node routed the message directly to the `event_queue` queue. Although the sender is connected to the `rabbit` node, it is the `instance3` node that is the owner of the `event_queue` queue and so it must receive all the messages that are designated for that queue. In that regard the queue will have pushed messages to the receiver even if it was subscribed to another node (e.g. `instance1`) that was not the owner of the queue.

Let's see what would happen in the scenario of a node failure:

- The **rabbit** node fails – in that case the sender will not be able to send a message. If however we had specified at least one more node that was running when creating the RabbitMQ connection from the subscriber, then the message would have been sent to that node:

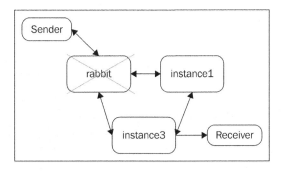

- The **instance1** node fails – nothing will happen in that case. The sender and the receiver will continue to function as usual. If the event_queue was declared on that node (rather than **instance3**), then that would disconnect the receiver even if it was still connected on a running node:

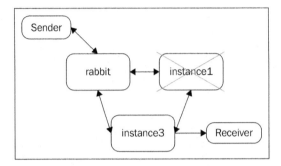

- The **instance3** node fails. That would disconnect the receiver even if more nodes were specified for the RabbitMQ connection from the receiver (and the receiver was connected to that node):

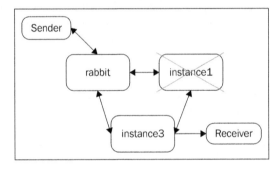

Based on several facts, it can be concluded that:

- RabbitMQ clustering support is targeted at horizontal scaling based on queue distribution among the nodes rather than high availability in the case of node failure
- The Java API does not support out-of-the box failover scenarios in terms of receiver/sender clients in the case of node failures; if a node fails, an exception is thrown that must be handled by the client and reconnection is not attempted

Case study: scaling the CSN

Over time, the users of the CSN increased rapidly and the workload of the system was increasing even more rapidly on a daily basis. It was estimated that this growth might cause issues with the single RabbitMQ broker instance, which essentially turned out to be a bottleneck.

That is why the team behind the CSN decided to introduce several new RabbitMQ instances installed on separate powerful servers and separate the queues from the v_events vhost on one node and the queues from the v_chat host on two other nodes:

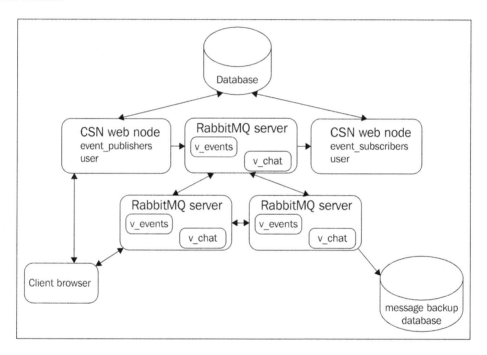

This not only improved the performance of the system (as shown by the benchmarks the CSN did over the new configuration) but also mitigated the risk of resource depletion on the single RabbitMQ server the system had.

Note that we are providing clustering support only on behalf of the message broker and this concept can be applied to the other components of the system.

Summary

In this chapter, we saw how to create a cluster of RabbitMQ nodes for the purpose of scaling out our broker. We saw how this allowed for the even distribution of queues on different nodes in the cluster, thus increasing storage capacity and performance in the cluster. We discussed what DISK and RAM nodes are and how they can be added and removed from a cluster; we also demonstrated how to connect to the cluster from a Java publisher/subscriber client and how a cluster tolerates failure on some of the nodes. Finally, we further extended the CSN with multiple RabbitMQ instances, forming a RabbitMQ cluster. The clustering mechanism supported by RabbitMQ has some drawbacks such as, for example, the lack of support for establishing high availability as a means of making image processing more reliable.

Exercises

1. Why do we store queue contents in a single node in the RabbitMQ cluster rather than replicating it over all nodes?

2. What types of cluster nodes does RabbitMQ support? What is the purpose of each of them?

3. What type of data is being sent between the nodes of a cluster?

4. How do nodes in a RabbitMQ cluster communicate?

5. How can you add a node to a cluster?

6. How can you remove a node from a cluster?

7. How can you check the cluster status?

8. What happens to the subscribers of a queue if its node goes down?

9. What considerations should be taken into account when deploying RabbitMQ cluster nodes on different machines in the network?

10. What drawbacks can you mention in the clustering mechanism provided by RabbitMQ?

5
High Availability

Even though messaging allows for a very loosely coupled type of communication, it is common in many scenarios that a large downtime or message loss are not acceptable, especially when guaranteed delivery must take place. In the previous chapter, we described how RabbitMQ supports clustering and how it focuses on queue scalability rather than providing high availability. In this chapter, we will further discover mechanisms for establishing high availability at the level of the message broker.

Topics covered in the chapter:

- Benefits of high availability
- High availability support in RabbitMQ
- Client high availability
- Case Study: Introducing high availability in CSN

Benefits of high availability

When we design and develop large systems that need to be up-and-running most of the time, we need to consider what would happen when a single component fails. This could be due to a hardware, network, or any other type of failure. Some systems, for example, have an **SLA (service level agreement)** that specifies a 99.99 percent uptime. In this regard, high availability should be considered for every such component that could turn out to be a bottleneck, including the message broker. This not only allows you to justify the SLAs (service level agreements) defined over your system, which increases confidence in its reliability, it also allows you to implement a system that minimizes as much as possible the impact of having a system that fails from time to time for a certain amount of time—at least until some manual intervention takes place in order to bring it up. This imposes the risk of losing money; the more users are impacted by a system failure, the more likely it is your SLAs oblige you to pay out. In reality, there are general solutions that allow you to provide high availability clusters for systems that do not have built-in support for creating such clusters. Luckily RabbitMQ provides mechanisms for that, as we will discover later in this chapter.

Moreover, we may want to perform upgrades without having to disrupt users of our system or backup data while the system is running.

High availability may be considered when:

- A connection fails (for example, due to a network/node failure). In that case, your client, either a publisher or a consumer, must be able to reconnect automatically to the cluster. You can use a load balancer that provides capabilities for detecting node failures or extending your client with support for reconnection to the cluster.

- A node fails. In that case, other nodes in the cluster should be able to take over the processing of messages in the cluster. There are various cluster topologies that allow for the implementation of high availability in a cluster. One is an active/active topology, where all nodes can take over the load for a failed node. Another type is an active/passive topology, where there are some passive nodes that can become active and take over the load for a failed node. There are yet other variations that are derived on the basis of these, considering the number of passive nodes available, or passivating nodes, when failed nodes become available again.

High availability support in RabbitMQ

RabbitMQ provides an extension of the default clustering mechanism that allows the replication of the contents of a queue over one or more nodes. It takes the active-active approach for establishing a highly available cluster, and you can select how many nodes to replicate a queue in a master-slave configuration (one node is designated as the master and all other nodes as the slaves):

- Replicate to all nodes in the cluster
- Replicate to a certain number of nodes in the cluster
- Replicate to certain nodes in the cluster (specified as a list of node names)

In terms of RabbitMQ, this extension is called mirrored queues.

Note that there is an opportunity to establish an active-passive RabbitMQ cluster using helper technologies that allow you to use redundant servers in order to establish that type of clustering; this was the preferred approach in most production scenarios before built-in support for mirrored queues was provided. However, mirrored queues are now the preferred approach since they are way faster and easier to configure than custom active-passive high availability configurations using third-party solutions. However, they inherit the drawbacks of the RabbitMQ built-in clustering mechanism on top of which they step:

- It cannot be applied across instances in distant locations (for example, datacenters in different regions in the world) due to the fact that it is very sensitive to latency issues. Such issues cause communication failures in the cluster. One solution could be to ensure that only high-bandwidth leased lines are available across the datacenters, thus eliminating the risk of latency problems.

- Even if a queue on a node is marked as durable, its contents cannot be directly copied over to another node in case the current one fails unless the mirrored queue policy you define matches the queue name. You should make sure that any new durable queues you add to the cluster (and need to be mirrored) are matched by a proper policy that specifies the nodes on which to replicate the contents of that queue. Otherwise, if no policy is in effect and if the node on which the durable queue is defined fails, then it should be restored again in order to be able to use that queue.

Having regard to the fact that RabbitMQ clustering is not proper for nodes over a WAN, queue mirroring must be supported with additional mechanisms that provide such distribution of queue contents. The federation and shovel plugins come to the rescue in that scenario. The federation plugin allows you to replicate messages between exchanges or between queues, while the shovel plugin allows you to send messages from a queue in one broker instance to an exchange in another broker instance. Apart from the fact that this provides a mechanism for establishing custom message broker topologies, it provides for a more resilient mechanism for communication between instances in an unreliable network environment, and also the possibility of running different versions of the RabbitMQ broker on each instance. Moreover, the different instances remain completely independent of each other.

In regard to the fact that there is a policy matching each queue we want to mirror, we must always consider testing either manually or automatically that our setup is correct by intentionally bringing down one or more nodes.

Mirrored queues

The steps for creating a mirrored queue are pretty straight-forward based on the fact that we already know how to configure a RabbitMQ cluster:

- Create the RabbitMQ cluster
- Create the mirroring policy over the particular queue from the cluster (this can be done from any node in the cluster)

The node on which the queue is created becomes the master and all other nodes matched by the mirroring policy become the slaves. When the master node fails then one of the slave nodes is designated as the new master; typically, this is the eldest slave node. The following diagram outlines a node with three nodes (the one we already described when we discussed clustering) and one mirrored queue called `mirrored_queue` defined on the rabbit node:

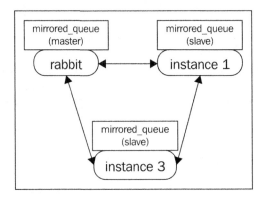

Assuming the `rabbit` node is already running, we will add the `instance1` DISK node (that persists metadata on disk) and the `instance3` RAM node (that persists metadata in-memory) to the cluster in the same way we did in the previous chapter:

```
set RABBITMQ_NODENAME=instance1 & set RABBITMQ_NODE_PORT=5701
&  rabbitmq-server -detached
rabbitmqctl -n instance1 stop_app
rabbitmqctl -n instance1 join_cluster rabbit@DOMAIN
rabbitmqctl -n instance1 start_app
set RABBITMQ_NODENAME=instance3 &  set RABBITMQ_NODE_PORT=5703 &
rabbitmq-server -detached
rabbitmqctl -n instance3 stop_app
rabbitmqctl -n instance3 join_cluster --ram rabbit@DOMAIN
rabbitmqctl -n instance3 start_app
```

Let's declare the `mirrored_queue` on the `instance1` node:

```
rabbitmqadmin.py declare queue name="mirrored_queue"
```

And finally let's make the queue mirrored on all nodes:

```
rabbitmqctl set_policy ha-all "mirrored_queue" "{""ha-mode"":""all""}"
```

If you go to the RabbitMQ management console and click on the **Queues** tab you will notice that `mirrored_queue` now has a +2 under node, indicating that there are two slaves, and under **Features** you can see a `ha-all` feature, which indicates the mirrored queue policy:

	Overview				Messages			Message rates			+/-
Virtual host	Name	Node	Features	State	Ready	Unacked	Total	incoming	deliver / get	ack	
/	**error_logs_dlx**	MARTIN	D	idle	0	0	0				
/	**mirrored_queue**	MARTIN +2	D ha-all	idle	0	0	0				
/	**test_queue**	MARTIN	D	idle	0	0	0				

If you click on `mirrored_queue` you see further information about the queue along with the slave nodes on which the queue is mirrored:

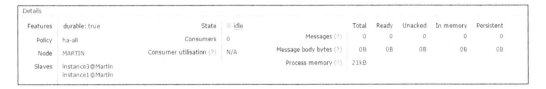

Each time a message is sent to a node in the RabbitMQ cluster, the channel routes the message directly to the master node, which passes it over to the slave instances. However in the event a new slave is created for the queue (for example, if a new node is joined to the cluster and we have a mirrored queue policy that replicates queue contents over all nodes), then it must be synchronized with the already existing messages in the master queue. Another scenario when synchronization is necessary is when the node of a durable slave queue is shut down and later restored; in that case, the contents of the durable queue are cleared by RabbitMQ and it behaves as if a new slave is joined to the master that needs synchronization. The master queue blocks until it synchronizes with the slave(s). Synchronization must be triggered either manually (which is the default behavior) or automatically (which can be defined as part of the mirrored queue policy).

Let's assume we have added a new node to the cluster we have. In that case we have to trigger synchronization manually using the following command:

```
rabbitmqctl sync_queue mirrored_queue
```

If you don't want to perform synchronization each time a new slave joins you can reconfigure your policy as follows:

```
rabbitmqctl set_policy ha-all "mirrored_queue" "{""ha-mode"":""all"",
""ha-sync-mode"":""automatic""}"
```

You may be wondering whether replication of messages and queue synchronization impact the performance of the cluster; the short answer is, yes they do. However this performance hit can be minimized by carefully defining the topology of your cluster. Let's assume that we have a large cluster with several queues defined on each node and each queue is mirrored over all other nodes in the cluster. This implies a lot of communication between the nodes in the cluster, which may introduce severe delays in message senders or receivers. One strategy that can be incorporated in order to avoid this is to have only one slave queue. You can do this by defining that you only want to replicate messages to one (random) node using the following policy:

```
rabbitmqctl set_policy ha-exactly "mirrored_queue" "{""ha-
mode"":""exactly"",""ha-params"":2,""ha-sync-mode"":""automatic""}"
```

The ha-exactly policy replaces the ha-all policy in effect for the **mirrored_queue** queue (although both policies exist in the cluster metadata), as visible from the RabbitMQ management console:

Virtual host	Name	Node	Features	State	Ready	Unacked	Total	incoming	deliver / get	ack	+/-
			Overview			Messages			Message rates		
/	error_logs_dlx	MARTIN	D	idle	0	0	0				
/	mirrored_queue	MARTIN +1	D ha-exactly	idle	0	0	0	0.00/s	0.00/s		
/	test_queue	MARTIN	D	idle	0	0	0				

Details					Total	Ready	Unacked	In memory	Persistent
Features	durable: true	State	idle		0	0	0	0	0
Policy	ha-exactly	Consumers	0	Messages (?)					
Node	MARTIN	Consumer utilisation (?)	N/A	Message body bytes (?)	0B	0B	0B	0B	0B
Slaves	instance1@Martin			Process memory (?)	21kB				

The `instance1` node is selected by RabbitMQ as the slave queue node. If you want to specify a concrete node for that purpose (let's say `instance3`), you can set the following policy:

```
rabbitmqctl set_policy ha-by-name "mirrored_queue"
"{""ha-mode"":""nodes"",""ha-params"":[""rabbit@DOMAIN"",
""instance3@Domain""],""ha-sync-mode"":""automatic""}"
```

In that case, the rabbit node is designated as the master and the `instance3` node as the slave. You should be careful with the names you specify in the `nodes` policy (also consider case-sensitivity); RabbitMQ will ignore invalid nodes and set master/slave nodes wrongly. Moreover, if you specify nodes that do not contain the current master node (the node where the queue is originally created), the policy will enforce the first node synchronized with the master slave node in the list to become the new master. If no such node is present in the list, RabbitMQ will continue using the current master until a node from the list is synchronized with it. You should be careful when changing mirroring policies and having unsynchronized slaves; this may cause unexpected behavior. Consider the following scenario where the master queue on the `rabbit` node has two messages that must be synchronized with the slaves on the other two nodes (`instance1` and `instance3`):

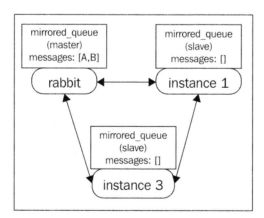

If the master queue node (in this case rabbit) fails, then RabbitMQ will try to elect a new master from one of the synchronized slaves (for example, from new or restored nodes that joined the cluster). Since we don't have such a slave, RabbitMQ will behave as if there are no slaves and processing on that queue will fail. If we don't want that to happen, we can additionally set the `ha-promote-on-shutdown` parameter to `always` on the mirroring policy; this will, however, impose the risk of losing messages in regard to the increased degree of high availability.

Mirrored queues are great for establishing high availability. However, the following questions remain open due to the fact that mirrored queues make use of the RabbitMQ clustering mechanism:

- How can we establish high availability over long distances since the clustering mechanism is not cooperative over the WAN?

- How can we upgrade cluster nodes both in terms of Erlang and RabbitMQ versions?

- How can we create a cluster of geographically distributed RabbitMQ clusters?

The Federation and Shovel plugins provide the answers to the preceding questions.

Federation plugin

The RabbitMQ federation plugin allows messages to be sent from an exchange in one host to an exchange in another or from a queue in one host to a queue in another. This is done by upstream links defined over the federated exchanges/queues in the upstream host (the host that receives the messages). The mechanism provided by the Federation plugin is not dependent upon RabbitMQ clustering but is cooperative with it, meaning that messages can be federated between exchanges or queues in different clusters. The Federation plugin must be enabled on the RabbitMQ nodes that participate in the message federation. All nodes in a RabbitMQ cluster must have the Federation plugin enabled in case replication of messages using the plugin happens between RabbitMQ clusters. To enable the plugin on a particular node execute the following command:

```
rabbitmq-plugins enable rabbitmq_federation
rabbitmq-plugins enable rabbitmq_federation_management
```

The `rabbitmq_federation_management` plugin enables management of the federation uplinks from the RabbitMQ management console.

Let's assume that we want to create a federated exchange and a federated queue defined in a new three-node cluster that link respectively to an upstream exchange and an upstream queue in our existing three-node cluster, as shown in the following diagram:

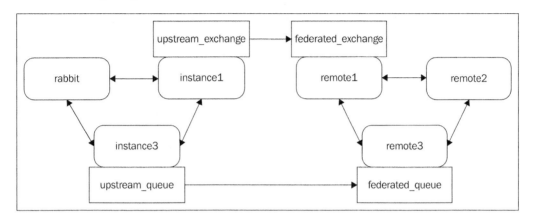

The following commands define our new local cluster:

```
set RABBITMQ_NODENAME=remote1 &
set RABBITMQ_NODE_PORT=5711 &
set RABBITMQ_SERVER_START_ARGS=-rabbitmq_management listener
[{port,55555}] &
rabbitmq-server.bat -detached
rabbitmq-plugins.bat -n remote1 enable rabbitmq_management
rabbitmq-plugins.bat -n remote2 disable rabbitmq_management
rabbitmq-plugins.bat -n remote3 disable rabbitmq_management
set RABBITMQ_NODENAME=remote2 &
set RABBITMQ_NODE_PORT=5712 &
rabbitmq-server.bat -detached
rabbitmqctl.bat -n remote2 stop_app
rabbitmqctl.bat -n remote2 join_cluster remote1@Martin
rabbitmqctl.bat -n remote2 start_app
set RABBITMQ_NODENAME=remote3 &
set RABBITMQ_NODE_PORT=5713 &
rabbitmq-server.bat -detached
rabbitmqctl.bat -n remote3 stop_app
rabbitmqctl.bat -n remote3 join_cluster remote1@Martin
rabbitmqctl.bat -n remote3 start_app
```

Essentially, the steps we perform in order to start a second cluster on a local machine are as follows:

- We start the `remote1` node and specify additionally `RABBITMQ_SERVER_START_ARGS`, which specifies the port on which we want to start the RabbitMQ management plugin (we are already using the management plugin for the initial cluster on default port 15672 and so we won't be able to enable its use for the management plugin UI in the second cluster). Another option is to specify a different configuration file for the `remote1` node before starting it using the `RABBITMQ_CONFIG_FILE` environment variable and specify the management plugin port inside that specific node configuration file.

- We enable the management plugin on the `remote1` node.

- We disable the management plugin on the `remote2` and `remote3` nodes (this is just a precaution in case RabbitMQ tries to start the management plugin by default on the nodes). Note that so far we have been using the default `enabled_plugins` file that stores the configuration of each plugin that must be enabled and so far we have been modifying the file using the `rabbitmq-plugins` utility before starting each node. However, it is better to specify a separated `enabled_plugins` file for each node, which can be achieved by setting the `RABBITMQ_ENABLED_PLUGINS_FILE` environment variable prior to starting each RabbitMQ node.

- We start the `remote2` and `remote3` nodes and join them in the same cluster using the `remote1` node in the usual manner we use to set up a cluster.

We need to enable the Federation plugin on the nodes in the cluster, create the upstream links, and set the proper federation policies on the `remote1` and `remote3` nodes, as shown in the preceding diagram. You can think of the later process as creating a "subscription" from the `federated_exchange` exchange in the remote cluster to the `upstream_exchange` in the initial cluster and a "subscription" from the `federated_queue` queue in the remote cluster to the `upstream_queue` queue in the initial cluster. The following enables the Federation plugin on the `remote3` node in the remote cluster:

```
rabbitmq-plugins -n remote1 enable rabbitmq_federation
rabbitmq-plugins -n remote1 enable rabbitmq_federation_management
```

To verify the cluster is successfully created, try opening `http://localhost:55555` and verify that you see the three cluster nodes in the management UI:

Name	File descriptors (?)	Socket descriptors (?)	Erlang processes	Memory	Disk space	Info	+/-
remote1@Martin	2 7280 available	201 1048576 available	43MB 3.2GB high watermark	66GB 48MB low watermark	Disc 4 Stats	
remote2@Martin	2 7280 available	156 1048576 available	41MB 3.2GB high watermark	66GB 48MB low watermark	Disc 3	
remote3@Martin	2 7280 available	157 1048576 available	38MB 3.2GB high watermark	66GB 48MB low watermark	Disc 3	

Let's define the exchanges and clusters in our clusters. We will define the exchanges as direct and bind additionally the `federated_queue` queue refined in the `remote3` node to the `federated_exchange` exchange defined in the `remote1` node:

```
rabbitmqadmin.py -N instance1 declare exchange name=upstream_exchange
type=direct
rabbitmqadmin.py -N instance3 declare queue name=upstream_queue
durable=false
rabbitmqadmin.py -N remote1 -P 55555 declare exchange name=federated_
exchange type=direct
rabbitmqadmin.py -N remote3 -P 55555 declare queue name=federated_
queue durable=false
rabbitmqadmin.py -N remote1 -P 55555 declare binding source=federated_
exchange destination=federated_queue routing_key=federated
```

Note that when creating the nodes using the `rabbitmqadmin` utility, we must specify the port of the RabbitMQ management plugin (here, 55555) since the utility uses the HTTP API of the management plugin. If we omit the port, the items will be created in the first cluster (since the default management plugin port of 15672 is used).

The final configuration we should make is to actually create the federation links by creating upstreams in the remote cluster and binding them to the target federated exchange or queue using policies:

```
rabbitmqctl -n remote1 set_parameter federation-upstream upstream
"{""uri"":""amqp://localhost:5672"",""expires"":3600000,
""exchange"":""upstream_exchange"", ""queue"":""upstream_queue""}"

rabbitmqctl -n remote1 set_policy federate-exchange
--apply-to exchanges "federated_exchange"
"{""federation-upstream"":""upstream""}"

rabbitmqctl -n remote1 set_policy federate-queue
--apply-to queues "federated_queue"
"{""federation-upstream"":""upstream""}"
```

We first create an upstream that points to the `rabbit` node in the first cluster (`amqp://localhost:5672`) and specifies `upstream_exchange` and `upstream_queue` as an upstream exchange and a queue. We can omit them from the definition of the upstream link, but in that case the policy would expect that their names should match those of the federated exchange and queue. After that, we define a federation policy for the `federated_exchange` that references the upstream link (thus retrieving messages from the `upstream_exchange`). Lastly, we define a policy for the `federated_queue` that references the upstream link (thus retrieving messages from the upstream exchange).

You may be wondering how the federation link authenticates against the upstream cluster or how we specify a vhost in which our upstream exchanges and queues reside. The answer to both of these question is related to the capabilities of the amqp URI scheme. We can additionally provide a username and password along with the vhost; by default, the `guest` user and the default vhost are assumed by the federation links.

We have already enabled the `federation_management_agent` on the remote cluster so we can observe the federation configuration in the management UI. If we navigate to `Federation Upstreams` under the `Admin` tab, we can see what federation upstreams we have configured, along with the attributes we have assigned to them (in our particular case a one-hour buffer for queuing messages from the upstream):

Federation Upstreams

▼ Upstreams

Name	URI	Expiry	Message TTL	Max Hops	Prefetch Count	Reconnect Delay	Ack mode	Trust User-ID
upstream	amqp://localhost:5672	3600000ms					?	?

▶ **Add a new upstream**

▶ **URI examples**

We can also check the status of the federation links from **Federation Status** under the **Admin** tab:

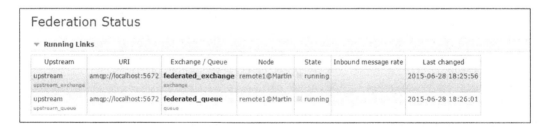

Federation Status

▼ Running Links

Upstream	URI	Exchange / Queue	Node	State	Inbound message rate	Last changed
upstream upstream_exchange	amqp://localhost:5672	**federated_exchange** exchange	remote1@Martin	running		2015-06-28 18:25:56
upstream upstream_queue	amqp://localhost:5672	**federated_queue** queue	remote1@Martin	running		2015-06-28 18:26:01

If we navigate to the **Exchanges** tab, we will observe the `federate-exchange` policy present as a feature on our `federated_exchange` exchange:

Name	Type	Features	Message rate in	Message rate out	+/-
(AMQP default)	direct	D			
amq.direct	direct	D			
amq.fanout	fanout	D			
amq.headers	headers	D			
amq.match	headers	D			
amq.rabbitmq.log	topic	D I			
amq.rabbitmq.trace	topic	D I			
amq.topic	topic	D			
federated_exchange	direct	D federate-exchange			

If we navigate to the **Queues** tab we will observe similar behavior for the `federated_queue` queue:

	Overview				Messages			Message rates		+/-
Name	Node	Features	State	Ready	Unacked	Total	incoming	deliver / get	ack	
federated_queue	remote1@Martin	federate-queue	idle	0	0	0				

If we navigate to the management UI of the first cluster (running on port `15672`) we will observe that a generic exchange and queue are created for the exchange federation link in the upstream cluster configuration:

Name	Type	Features	Message rate in	Message rate out	+/-
(AMQP default)	direct	D			
amq.direct	direct	D			
amq.fanout	fanout	D			
amq.headers	headers	D			
amq.match	headers	D			
amq.rabbitmq.log	topic	D I			
amq.rabbitmq.trace	topic	D I			
amq.topic	topic	D			
federation: upstream_exchange -> remote1@Martin:federated_exchange B	x-federation-upstream	D AD I Args			
upstream_exchange	direct	D			

	Overview				Messages			Message rates		+/-
Name	Node	Features	State	Ready	Unacked	Total	incoming	deliver / get	ack	
federation: upstream_exchange -> remote1@Martin:federated_exchange	MARTIN	D Exp Args	idle	0	0	0				
upstream_queue	MARTIN		idle	0	0	0				

In order to verify that the federation links work, we will send two messages, one to the `upstream_exchange` with the `federated` binding key (earlier we created a binding with that key between `federated_exchange` and `federated_queue`) and one to the default exchange with the `upstream_queue` key:

```
rabbitmqadmin.py publish exchange=upstream_exchange
routing_key=federated payload="first test message"
rabbitmqadmin.py publish exchange=amq.default
routing_key=upstream_queue payload="second test message"
```

If you subscribe to the `federated_queue` in the remote cluster using the ClusterReceiver Java class from the previous chapter, you will notice that in both cases the subscriber instance receives the test messages. In the first case, the `upstream_exchange` exchange sends the message to the `federated_exchange` exchange in the remove cluster and the `federated_exchange` exchange routes the message to the `federated_queue` queue, using the `federated` routing key matching the binding key defined between the exchange and the queue in the remote cluster. In the second case, the federated link sends the message from the `upstream_queue` queue directly to the `federated_queue`.

You can play around with the cluster by bringing down nodes from one of the clusters and investigating how the exchange/queue federation behaves in certain scenarios; since the federation plugin is aware of RabbitMQ clusters, it will try to migrate exchange/queue federation links in case a node in the upstream/downstream cluster fails. What would happen if the `instance3` node that is the node for the `upstream_queue` queue fails? If we bring down the node and send the two test messages again we will find that both of them arrive successfully at the `federated_queue` queue.

Shovel plugin

The Federation plugin is not the only mechanism that allows for successfully sending messages between RabbitMQ instances over the WAN. The shovel plugin can be used to send a message from a queue defined in a single RabbitMQ instance to an exchange defined in another RabbitMQ instance located possibly in a different geographic location. This means that the shovel plugin can also be used to transfer messages over the WAN and moreover, it is also cooperative in clustered configurations. The Shovel plugin works at a lower level than the Federation plugin and can be defined either statically (in the RabbitMQ configuration file) or dynamically, via parameters similarly to how federation upstreams are created. Dynamic shovels are a newer addition to the Shovel plugin (introduced with the release 3.3.0 of RabbitMQ). Having regard to static shovels, which provide only the option to send messages from a source queue to a destination exchange, dynamic shovels provide all scenarios for queue/exchange-to-queue/exchange message sending in addition to a simplified configuration.

In order to use the Shovel plugin you must enable it on the target nodes along with the management plugin extensions (if needed). The following commands enable a dynamic shovel between the `upstream_queue` in the source cluster and the `federated_exchange` in the target cluster (the same configuration can be achieved using static shovels but without the benefits of dynamic configuration):

```
rabbitmq-plugins -n remote1 enable rabbitmq_shovel
rabbitmq-plugins -n rabbit enable rabbitmq_shovel_management

rabbitmqctl -n remote1 set_parameter shovel test_shovel
"{""src-uri"": ""amqp://localhost:5672"", ""src-queue"": ""upstream_
queue"", ""dest-uri"": ""amqp://localhost:5712"", ""dest-exchange"":
""federated_exchange""}"
```

If you open `localhost:55555` (the management web interface for the remote cluster) in the browser and navigate to **Shovel Management**, when clicking the **Admin** tab you will notice that there is one dynamic shovel configured:

You can also inspect the status of the shovel when navigating to the **Shovel Status** under the **Admin** tab and verify that the shovel is up-and-running:

In fact, we can specify the dynamic shovel in the upstream cluster with regard to the federation plugin where we need to specify the upstreams and the federation policies in the node where the federated exchanges/queues reside.

To verify that the shovel works, we can create a second binding between the federation_upstream and the federation_queue with a binding key of upstream_queue, and send a test message to the default exchange in the first cluster (the routing key of the message is passed along from the upstream_queue queue in the source cluster to the federated_exchange exchange in the destination cluster):

```
rabbitmqadmin.py -N remote1 -P 55555 declare binding source=federated_
exchange destination=federated_queue routing_key=upstream_queue
rabbitmqadmin.py publish exchange=amq.default
routing_key=upstream_queue payload="second test message"
```

If we subscribe to the federation_queue queue, we will notice that the message is successfully received.

The following table provides a summary of the different options supported by the Federation and Shovel plugins:

source \ destination	exchange	queue
exchange	federation dynamic shovel	dynamic shovel
queue	static shovel dynamic shovel	federation dynamic shovel

Reliable delivery

So far we have been looking at high availability mostly in terms of node redundancy. What about network connections? Network failures introduce another degree of uncertainty when transferring messages via a single RabbitMQ node or an entire cluster of nodes. Let's refer to the cluster we created originally:

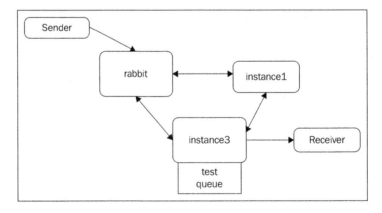

What happens if the sender sends a message to the default exchange with a key of test (the name of the test queue defined in instance3) By default, both publisher and subscriber do not expect any acknowledgements. Remember that performance is by default the target priority for the broker. Here is what happens:

- The sender sends a message and does not await a confirmation that the broker has successfully processed the message (delivered it to the test queue)

- The broker receives the message and routes it to the test queue, which may or may not persist it on disk or replicate it among the other nodes in the cluster (depending on how durability and mirroring are configured)

- The broker sends the message to the receiver without awaiting acknowledgement from the receiver (by default the queue is created with autoAck=true, meaning that the message is discarded from the queue once sent to the receiver without awaiting a confirmation)

The preceding message flow does not take into account reliable delivery. In particular:

- If the sender has sent the message (the first step is completed) but the broker instance fails while processing the message, then the message is lost and publishing is unsuccessful.

- If however the message is successfully sent to the broker (the second step is completed) and the test queue is created with autoAck=false, then the receiver must send an acknowledgement/rejection of the message. Only when the queue receives an explicit acknowledgement from the receiver will it discard the message. If the receiver gets the message but the broker node that hosts the queue fails before processing the acknowledgement from the queue, then it may send the message a second time to the receiver once up-and-running again (assuming the message is lost and hence consumption is unsuccessful).

In both of the preceding scenarios we need a mechanism that will guarantee that publishing/acknowledging messages is successful at the broker. This is possible via AMQP transactions.

AMQP transactions

The AMQP 0-9-1 specification defines the `tx` class of protocol operation that allows us to establish transactions with the broker:

- `tx.select`, for starting a transaction with the broker
- `tx.commit`, for committing a transaction at the broker
- `tx.rollback`, for rolling back a transaction at the broker

A transaction is initiated by the client using the `tx.select` AMQP command and then committed or rolled-back depending on the particular use case. The `TransactionalSender` class provides an example of a sender that uses transactions (queue, exchange, or binding declarations are omitted for the sake of simplicity):

```
import java.io.IOException;
import org.slf4j.Logger;
import org.slf4j.LoggerFactory;
import com.rabbitmq.client.Channel;
import com.rabbitmq.client.Connection;
import com.rabbitmq.client.ConnectionFactory;



public class TransactionalSender {

    private final static Logger LOGGER =
    LoggerFactory.getLogger(TransactionalSender.class);

    public void send(String exchange, String key, String message){
        Connection connection = null;
        Channel channel = null;
        try {
            ConnectionFactory factory =
             new ConnectionFactory();
            factory.setHost("localhost");
            connection = factory.newConnection();
            channel = connection.createChannel();

            channel.txSelect();channel.basicPublish(exchange, key,
null,
                 message.getBytes());
            channel.txCommit();
        } catch (IOException e) {
            LOGGER.error(e.getMessage(), e);
            if (channel != null) {
```

```
                        try {
                            channel.txRollback();
                        } catch (IOException re) {
                            LOGGER.error("Rollback failed: " +
re.getMessage(), re);
                        }
                    }
                } finally {
                    if(connection != null) {
                        try {
                            connection.close();
                        } catch (IOException e) {
                        LOGGER.warn("Failed to close connection: " +
                            e.getMessage(), e);
                        }
                    }
                }
            }
        }
    }
```

In the preceding example, you can publish as many messages as you want between `txSelect()` and `txCommit()` and all of them are committed/rolled back at once. This means that AMQP transactions are very suitable for creating batch publishing of messages. In practice, this can improve the performance of our application if we need to guarantee that messages are successfully processed by the broker and we decide to use AMQP transactions for the purpose.

The following example demonstrations using AMQP transactions with subscriber acknowledgements:

```java
import java.io.IOException;
import org.slf4j.Logger;
import org.slf4j.LoggerFactory;
import com.rabbitmq.client.Channel;
import com.rabbitmq.client.Connection;
import com.rabbitmq.client.ConnectionFactory;
import com.rabbitmq.client.ConsumerCancelledException;
import com.rabbitmq.client.QueueingConsumer;
import com.rabbitmq.client.ShutdownSignalException;

public class TransactionalReceiver {

    private final static Logger LOGGER = LoggerFactory.
        getLogger(TransactionalReceiver.class);
```

```
    private static final String REQUEST_QUEUE = "tx_queue";

public void receive() {
    Connection connection = null;
    Channel channel = null;
    try {
        ConnectionFactory factory = new ConnectionFactory();
        factory.setHost("localhost");
        connection = factory.newConnection();
        channel = connection.createChannel();
QueueingConsumer consumer = new QueueingConsumer(channel);
        channel.basicConsume(REQUEST_QUEUE, false, consumer);
        QueueingConsumer.Delivery delivery =
consumer.nextDelivery();
        String message = new String(delivery.getBody());
        LOGGER.info("Request received: " + message);
        channel.txSelect();
        channel.basicAck(delivery.getEnvelope().getDeliveryTag(),
            false);
        channel.txCommit();
    } catch (IOException e) {
        LOGGER.error(e.getMessage(), e);
        if (channel != null) {
            try {
                channel.txRollback();
            } catch (IOException re) {
LOGGER.error("Rollback failed: " + re.getMessage(), re);
            }
        }
    } catch (ShutdownSignalException e) {
        LOGGER.error(e.getMessage(), e);
    } catch (ConsumerCancelledException e) {
        LOGGER.error(e.getMessage(), e);
    } catch (InterruptedException e) {
        LOGGER.error(e.getMessage(), e);
    } finally {
        if(connection != null) {
            try {
                connection.close();
            } catch (IOException e) {
                LOGGER.warn("Failed to close
                    connection: " +
e.getMessage(), e);
```

```
                    }
                }
            }
        }
    }
```

In the preceding example, we set `autoAck` to false when we bind the consumer to the queue and then we use the basicAck method to acknowledge that the message is processed successfully by the consumer.

Publisher confirms

While AMQP transactions provide a reliable mechanism for ensuring that the broker has processed a message upon publishing, it is quite heavyweight. There are two reasons for this:

- Transactions make publishing messages synchronous; the publisher cannot send a message over the same channel until the previously sent message has been confirmed
- Transactions are onerous operations on their own.

For that reason, the broker introduces an extension called publisher confirms (not defined in the AMQP spec). Publisher confirms work by creating a channel in publish model, thus making the broker responsible for sending acknowledgements upon successful processing of messages over the channel. Moreover, confirms are asynchronous, meaning that multiple messages can be sent and confirmed independently by the broker. In order to enable publisher confirms you can modify the `TransactionalPublisher` class as follows:

- Use the confirmSelect() method instead of txSelect() on the channel in order to enable publisher confirms
- Register a handler for message acknowledgements/rejections from the broker

The following snippet demonstrates the preceding points:

```
channel.addConfirmListener(new ConfirmListener() {     public void
handleNack(long deliveryTag, boolean multiple) throws IOException {
        LOGGER.warn("Message(s) rejected.");
    }

    public void handleAck(long deliveryTag,      boolean multiple)
        throws IOException {
            LOGGER.warn("Message(s) confirmed.");
    }});

channel.confirmSelect();
channel.basicPublish(exchange, key, null, message.getBytes());
```

Client high availability

Now that we have seen how to establish high availability at the level of the broker along with some mechanisms to improve reliability when publishing/consuming messages, we have to explore what mechanisms we have to ensure client reliability in the event of broker failures.

Client reconnections

Later versions of the RabbitMQ Java client provide a mechanism for handling automatic recovery in the event of connection failures with the broker. In earlier versions of the client this has to be done manually or with the help of a wrapper library that provides recovery on top of an existing RabbitMQ client (there are various implementations in the public space). Recovery via the Java client API is enabled with a single line of code:

```
factory.setAutomaticRecoveryEnabled(true);
```

The preceding method invoked on a RabbitMQ connection factory does a number of things in the context of a publisher/consumer connection, such as reopening channels, recovering consumers, restoring connection/channel settings and listeners, and redeclaring queues/exchanges/bindings.

Load balancing

Another option you have in order to improve reliability upon connection to the broker is to use a hardware/software TCP load-balancer (such as HAProxy and Balance). It requires more configuration but you can manage the IP addresses of cluster nodes in the configuration of the load balancer rather than the configuration of the client. Apart from that, you get a mechanism for the even distribution of traffic among nodes in the cluster using the features provided by the TCP load balancer.

Case study: introducing high availability in CSN

With the increase in utilization of the CSN, it was decided to establish additional mechanisms that would allow a more resilient day-to-day usage of the CSN. The system was performing well but with no guarantees in respect of information loss. Since event propagation is considered a highly important concept in the normal operation of the CSN, message loss in that area was established as a major risk. For that reason, the team decided to apply additional mechanisms for minimizing that risk. In particular, the innovations that were introduced were:

- Support for automatic recovery in the CSN web and worker nodes and the browser plugin.

- Support for publisher confirms when sending messages from the web node.

- Additional remote RabbitMQ instance for the purpose of disaster recovery. The CSN web and worker nodes and the browser plugin were enhanced to take the remote instance into consideration upon automatic recovery (by extending those nodes with the address of the remote instance). The remote instance defined as upstream the nodes in the original RabbitMQ cluster, along with a policy for replication of all queues from the v_events vhost:

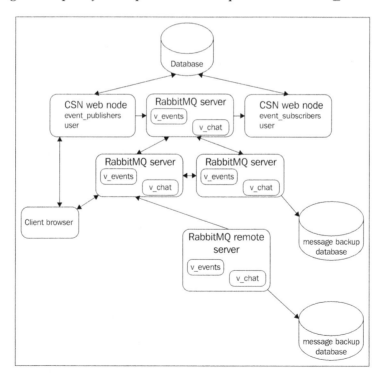

Summary

In this chapter, we saw how to extend the concept of RabbitMQ clustering with mirrored queues, which allow us to establish high availability at the level of the broker. Furthermore, we discussed additional mechanisms for improving reliability (in terms of connecting to the broker and processing messages such as AMQP transactions), publisher confirms, and client reconnections.

Exercises

1. How is high availability established?

2. How do mirrored queues work?

3. What is the Federation plugin used for?

4. How does the Federation plugin behave when used between exchanges/queues in clusters?

5. What is the Shovel plugin used for?

6. How can you ensure a message has been processed successfully by the broker upon publishing?

7. How can you establish high availability in terms of client connectivity to a RabbitMQ cluster?

6
Integrations

So far, we have been looking at what features does RabbitMQ provide in terms of fast and reliable message sending—from message patterns and broker administration to clustering and high availability. In this chapter, we will go further by providing an overview of how the broker integrates with other systems and how the other systems integrate with the broker.

The following topics will be covered in the chapter:

- Spring framework integrations
- Integration with ESBs
- Integration with databases
- RabbitMQ integrations
- RabbitMQ deployment options
- Testing RabbitMQ applications

Types of integrations

Let's take a look at the standard setup that we have been discussing so far (including a producer, consumer, and three-node RabbitMQ cluster):

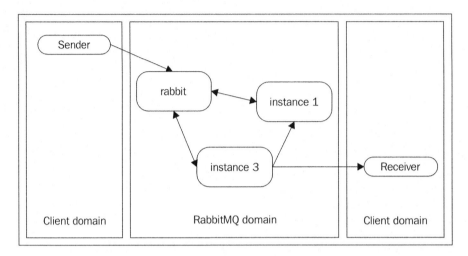

If we consider the client domain (publisher/subscriber), we can perform the following:

- We can use a client AMQP library written in any programming language (thus integrating RabbitMQ with a particular programming language). We are already using the out-of-the-box RabbitMQ Java client. As RabbitMQ supports a multitude of AMQP clients, you can use one that best suits your application or write your own AMQP client in your programming language of choice, if one is missing.

- We can use a wrapper library written on top of a client library. Many applications that use RabbitMQ as a message broker are deployed as part of a web or dependency injection container. For this reason, there are wrappers around the client libraries for different containers, such as the ones provided by the Spring framework and implemented on top of the RabbitMQ Java client library and Spring AMQP library.

If we consider the RabbitMQ domain (the RabbitMQ cluster), we can perform the following:

- We can send messages via other protocols such as STOMP, MQTT, or HTTP.

- We can send messages via AMQP from an **ESB** (**enterprise service bus**) such as Mule ESB or WSO2 that integrate with a number of other protocols.

- We can persist messages by subscribing to the broker directly from a database (either relational or NoSQL) using the utilities provided by the database rather than a separate application that subscribes to the broker and persists to the database. For example, this could be a PL/SQL stored procedure that subscribes directly to the message broker (in case of an Oracle relational database management system).

Spring framework

Many applications that are deployed along with a dependency injection container such as Spring make use of the additional utilities provided by the container in order to use a variety of features out of the box. In terms of RabbitMQ, these features are as follows:

- **Spring AMQP**: This provides you with an abstraction layer and core library on top of the AMQP protocol. The Spring RabbitMQ library uses it to provide utilities for interaction with the RabbitMQ message broker.

- **Spring Integration**: The framework provides an implementation of the enterprise integration patterns as defined by Gregor Hohpe and Bobby Wolfe in their book on this topic. As such, the Spring integration framework serves the purpose of providing a convenient Spring-based DSL for the configuration of an enterprise integration bus that enables different systems to communicate with each other. In this regard, the framework provides producer/consumer adapters for RabbitMQ.

- **Spring XD** (**extreme data**): The framework provides capabilities for easier handling and analytics on big data from a variety of sources—RabbitMQ message broker being one of them.

Spring AMQP

The Spring AMQP framework along with the more concrete Spring RabbitMQ support that builds on top of that framework provides the biggest portion of RabbitMQ in the Spring framework. There are three main building blocks behind Spring RabbitMQ:

- The **RabbitTemplate** class that provides a convenient utility to publish messages or subscribe to a RabbitMQ broker
- The **RabbitAdmin** class that provides a convenient utility to create/remove exchanges, queues, and bindings
- The message listener containers that provide a convenient mechanism to create asynchronous listeners that bind to a RabbitMQ message queue

Each of these can be used either directly or configured via a Spring XML or annotation-based configuration. In order to include the Spring Rabbit library in your application, you need to add the following Maven dependency to the pom.xml file of your project:

```
<dependency>
<groupId>org.springframework.amqp</groupId>
    <artifactId>spring-rabbit</artifactId>
    <version>1.4.5.RELEASE</version>
</dependency>
```

The following snippet demonstrates the use of the RabbitTemplate class to send a message to a queue named **sample-queue** via the default exchange:

```
CachingConnectionFactory factory = null;
try {
    factory = new CachingConnectionFactory("localhost");
    RabbitTemplate template = new RabbitTemplate(factory);
    template.convertAndSend("", "sample-queue",
"sample-queue test message!");
} finally {
    If(factory != null) {
        factory.destroy();
    }
}
```

Initially, we create an instance of the `CachingConnectionFactory` class provided by Spring RabbitMQ that, by default, caches a predefined number of channels (and is very convenient to use in a concurrent environment), but the cache mode can be set to cache connections rather than channels and the cache size of the factory can be changed as well. We can specify a number of additional properties on a `CachingConnectionFactory` instance such as the host and port against which to connect (or multiple addresses, in case of a RabbitMQ cluster), a virtual host, username, password, or even a different thread pool implementation (implementation of the Java ExecutorService, Spring-based or a custom one) used by the factory when it creates connections/channels. We then use `convertAndSend()` of the `RabbitTemplate` class to send a message by specifying an exchange and routing key. In the final block, we destroy the connection factory.

The following example demonstrates the use of the `RabbitAdmin` class to create a queue called **sample-queue** and bind it to an exchange called **sample-topic-exchange** using the **sample-key** binding key:

```
CachingConnectionFactory factory = new CachingConnectionFactory
("localhost");
RabbitAdmin admin = new RabbitAdmin(factory);
Queue queue = new Queue("sample-queue");
admin.declareQueue(queue);
TopicExchange exchange = new TopicExchange("sample-topic-exchange");
admin.declareExchange(exchange);
admin.declareBinding(BindingBuilder.bind(queue).
to(exchange).with("sample-key"));
factory.destroy();
```

The RabbitTemplate and `RabbitAdmin` classes are convenient utilities that allow you to send/retrieve messages from the broker and create broker items. If you want to listen asynchronously for messages sent to a queue, you can create one using a listener container as follows:

```
CachingConnectionFactory factory = new CachingConnectionFactory
("localhost");
SimpleMessageListenerContainer container = new SimpleMessageListener
Container(factory);
Object listener = new Object() {
public void handleMessage(String message) {
System.out.println("Message received: " + message);
    }
};
```

```
MessageListenerAdapter adapter = new MessageListenerAdapter(listener);
container.setMessageListener(adapter);
container.setQueueNames("sample-queue");
container.start();
```

First, we create `SimpleMessageListenerContainer` that is used to manage the listener's life cycle; it allows the listener to bind to more than one queue. Then we create an instance of the listener by supplying the `handleMessage()` method; we can also use an instance of the `MessageListener` interface from the `Spring AMQP` library in order to avoid the usage of `MessageListenerAdapter` from the preceding example. After we have set the listener and queue names on the listener container instance, we can bind the listener asynchronously using the `start()` method.

All of these examples demonstrate the use of the utilities provided by the Spring RabbitMQ library without using any additional Spring configuration.

We can decouple the configuration of `RabbitTemplate`, `RabbitAdmin`, and listener container instances using the Spring configuration. The additional benefit is that the source code becomes even more concise. The following sample Spring XML configuration file demonstrates how to configure the Spring RabbitMQ utilities:

```
<beans xmlns=http://www.springframework.org/schema/beans
xmlns:xsi="http://www.w3.org/2001/XMLSchema-instance"
xmlns:rabbit=http://www.springframework.org/schema/rabbit
xsi:schemaLocation="http://www.springframework.org/schema/rabbit
http://www.springframework.org/schema/rabbit/spring-rabbit.xsd
http://www.springframework.org/schema/beans
http://www.springframework.org/schema/beans/spring-beans.xsd">

<rabbit:connection-factory id="connectionFactory" host="localhost" />
<rabbit:template id="amqpTemplate" connection-factory="connection
Factory" exchange="" routing-key="sample-queue-spring"/>

<rabbit:admin connection-factory="connectionFactory" />
<rabbit:queue name="sample-queue-spring" />
<rabbit:topic-exchange name="sample-spring-exchange">
<rabbit:bindings>
<rabbit:binding queue="sample-queue-spring"
pattern="sample-key-spring" />
```

```
    </rabbit:bindings>
  </rabbit:topic-exchange>

  <rabbit:listener-container
      connection-factory="connectionFactory">
      <rabbit:listener ref="springListener" method="receiveMessage"
  queue-names="sample-queue-spring" />
  </rabbit:listener-container>
  <bean id="springListener" class="ContainerListenerSpringExample" />
</beans>
```

We first declare the connection factory instance and then use it to create a RabbitTemplate instance, RabbitAdmin instance, and listener container. The RabbitTemplate instance is configured to use the default exchange with a **sample-queue-spring** routing key by default. On the creation of a connection to the broker, a topic exchange called **sample-spring-exchange** will be defined. A new asynchronous listener that binds to the **sample-queue-spring** queue will be created.

Here is a sample usage of the RabbitTemplate class using the preceding configuration (Note that the asynchronous listener is also created and bound upon context initialization.):

```
AbstractApplicationContext context = new ClassPathXmlApplication
Context("configuration.xml");
RabbitTemplate template = context.getBean(RabbitTemplate.class);
template.convertAndSend("Sample Spring test message.");
context.destroy();
```

Spring Integration

The Spring integration framework provides support for RabbitMQ by means of proper adapters to send a message or subscribe to a queue. In order to use the Spring integration AMQP adapters, you have to include the following dependencies in the build configuration of your Maven project:

```
<dependency>
    <groupId>org.springframework.integration</groupId>
    <artifactId>spring-integration-core</artifactId>
    <version>4.0.4.RELEASE</version>
</dependency>
<dependency>
```

```
            <groupId>org.springframework.integration</groupId>
            <artifactId>spring-integration-amqp</artifactId>
            <version>4.0.4.RELEASE</version>
    </dependency>
```

We will implement the following simple Spring integration message bus:

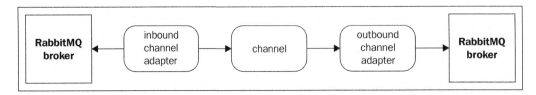

First, we subscribe to a queue in the RabbitMQ broker using a Spring integration
AMQP inbound channel adapter. The inbound channel adapter is bound to a Spring
integration channel that routes messages to a Spring integration AMQP outbound
channel adapter from where it is sent to a RabbitMQ message broker. (We will
use the same RabbitMQ broker as the one to which the inbound channel adapter
binds.) Note that the channel works with a common representation of a message—
the purpose of the adapters is to convert that representation to/from the AMQP
representation of a message. The following Spring configuration describes the
preceding components and the connection between them using the **test-queue** queue
as a source queue and the **test-destination-queue** queue as a destination queue:

```
<?xml version="1.0" encoding="UTF-8"?>
<beans:beans
xmlns=http://www.springframework.org/schema/
integrationxmlns:xsi=http://www.w3.org/2001/XMLSchema-
instancexmlns:beans=http://www.springframework.org/schema/
beans
xmlns:amqp=http://www.springframework.org/schema/integration/amqp
xmlns:rabbit=http://www.springframework.org/schema/rabbit
xmlns:context=http://www.springframework.org/schema/
contextxmlns:stream=http://www.springframework.org/schema/integration/
stream
xsi:schemaLocation="http://www.springframework.org/schema/beans
http://www.springframework.org/schema/beans/spring-beans.xsd
http://www.springframework.org/schema/context
http://www.springframework.org/schema/context/spring-context.xsd
http://www.springframework.org/schema/rabbit
http://www.springframework.org/schema/rabbit/spring-rabbit.xsd
http://www.springframework.org/schema/integration
```

```
http://www.springframework.org/schema/integration/spring-integration-
4.1.xsd
http://www.springframework.org/schema/integration/stream
http://www.springframework.org/schema/integration/stream/spring-
integration-stream-4.1.xsd
http://www.springframework.org/schema/integration/amqp
http://www.springframework.org/schema/integration/amqp/spring-
integration-amqp.xsd">
    <rabbit:connection-factory id="connectionFactory"
host="localhost" />
    <channel id="test-channel" />

    <rabbit:queue name="test-queue" />
    <rabbit:queue name="test-destination-queue" />

    <rabbit:template id="amqpTemplate"
connection-factory="connectionFactory"
exchange="" routing-key="test-queue" />
    <rabbit:admin connection-factory="connectionFactory" />

    <amqp:inbound-channel-adapter channel="test-channel"
queue-names="test-queue" connection-factory="connectionFactory" />

    <amqp:outbound-channel-adapter channel="test-channel"
exchange-name="" routing-key="test-destination-queue"
amqp-template="amqpTemplate" />

    <rabbit:connection-factory id="connectionFactory"
host="localhost" />
</beans:beans>
```

The following example demonstrates the use of the preceding configuration to send a message to the **test-queue** queue that is delivered via the Spring integration channel to the **test-destination-queue** queue:

```
AbstractApplicationContext context =
new ClassPathXmlApplicationContext(
"configuration-int.xml");
RabbitTemplate template = context.
getBean(RabbitTemplate.class);
template.convertAndSend("test message ...");
```

Integration with ESBs

Various ESBs also provide features to integrate with a RabbitMQ message broker. In the previous example, we saw how to use Spring integration as an ESB that provides RabbitMQ adapters. In the following section, we will take a look at the Mule and WSO2 ESBs that also provide integration with RabbitMQ.

Mule ESB

The Mule ESB provides you with a runtime and development environment based on the Eclipse IDE called **Anypoint Studio** that allows you to create integration workflows easily using either a graphical editor or directly from the XML configuration file of your Mule ESB project. The **AnypointStudio** comes with a preinstalled runtime of the Mule ESB enterprise edition but you can also set up a community edition of MuleESB with the development studio. The first step is to download the trial version of the AnypointStudio from the official MuleSoft website and install it. Start the studio and create a new project by clicking on the **Create a Project** button:

Then specify the name and Maven settings for the new project:

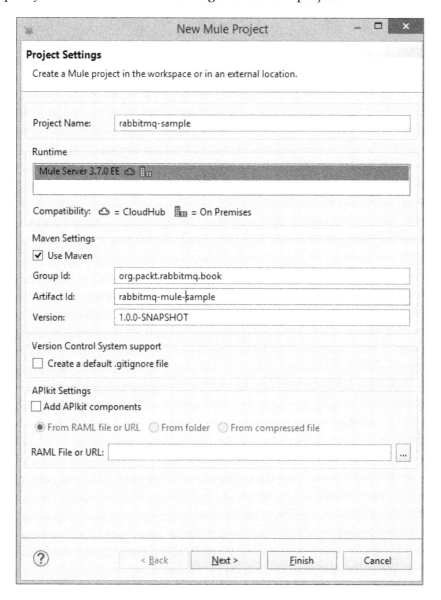

Specify the location and JDK version of your project; specify an already installed JDK by clicking on the `Configure JREs` link, and finally, click on the **Finish** button:

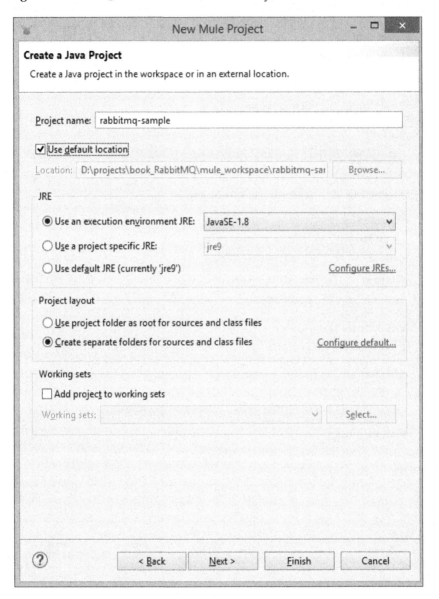

After you create the new Mule project, you will notice that a graphical editor appears, where you can specify the integration flow of your application using the drag-and-drop items on the right-hand side of the editor. You can see a number of preinstalled connectors on the right-hand side. However, an AMQP/RabbitMQ connector is missing and must be installed separately. To install this, navigate to **Help -> Install New Software ...** in the AnypointStudio; select `Anypoint Connectors Update Site` from the **Work With** drop down; type in the Search **AMQP** and select **Mule AMQP Transport**, as shown in the following screenshot:

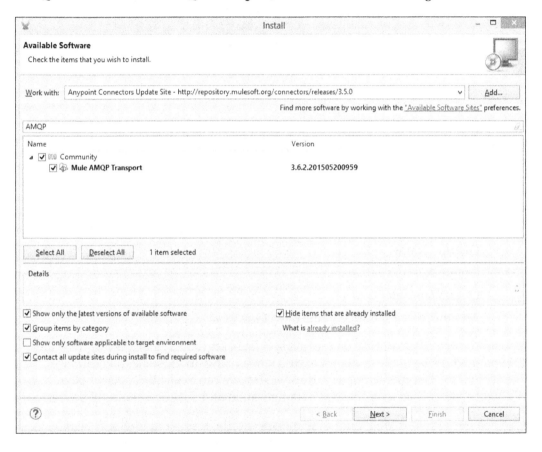

We will create the same flow that we created with Spring integration without the need to specify a channel. (It is implicitly represented by the Mule ESB.) From the **Endpoints** section, drag and drop an **AMQP-0-9** item to the workspace. Select a second **AMQP-0-9** item and drag-and-drop it in the **Process** area of the workspace, next to the first item:

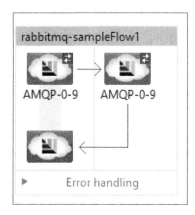

Double-click on the flow window that contains the two items and change the name to `rabbitmq-sample-flow`. Click on the first AMQP endpoint and specify the following (this will be our inbound endpoint that will subscribe to the `test-queue` queue):

- **Display Name**: `rabbitmq-inbound-endpoint`
- **Queue Name**: `test-queue`
- **Queue Durable**: `enabled`
- **Advanced -> Exchange Patterns -> One Way**: `default`

You need to specify explicitly on the queue-related attributes so that Mule precreates the specified queue in the endpoint in case it is missing. In the preceding case, we specify that the **test-queue** queue is durable (but we can explicitly specify queue durability as `false` in the Mule XML configuration and the queue will still be created).

Click on the second AMQP endpoint and specify the following (this will be our outbound endpoint that will send messages to the **test-destination-queue** queue):

- **Display Name**: `rabbitmq-outbound-endpoint`
- **Queue Name**: `test-destination-queue`
- **Routing Key**: `test-destination-queue`
- **Queue Durable**: `enabled`
- **Advanced -> Exchange Patterns -> One Way**: `default`

Apart from the endpoints, you also need to specify an AMQP connector configuration in your Mule configuration, and specify it for both endpoints using the **connector-ref** attribute so that they connect to the designated RabbitMQ broker. The Mule configuration for the projects is the following:

```
<?xml version="1.0" encoding="UTF-8"?>
<mule xmlns:tracking="http://www.mulesoft.org/schema/mule/ee/tracking"
xmlns:http="http://www.mulesoft.org/schema/mule/http"
xmlns:amqp="http://www.mulesoft.org/schema/mule/amqp" xmlns="http://
www.mulesoft.org/schema/mule/core" xmlns:doc="http://www.mulesoft.org/
schema/mule/documentation"
xmlns:spring="http://www.springframework.org/schema/beans"
version="EE-3.7.0"
xmlns:xsi="http://www.w3.org/2001/XMLSchema-instance"
xsi:schemaLocation="http://www.mulesoft.org/schema/mule/http http://
www.mulesoft.org/schema/mule/http/3.1/mule-http.xsd
http://www.mulesoft.org/schema/mule/core http://www.mulesoft.org/
schema/mule/core/3.1/mule.xsd
http://www.mulesoft.org/schema/mule/amqp http://www.mulesoft.org/
schema/mule/amqp/3.1/mule-amqp.xsd
http://www.mulesoft.org/schema/mule/ee/tracking http://www.mulesoft.
org/schema/mule/ee/tracking/3.1/mule-tracking-ee.xsd
http://www.springframework.org/schema/beans http://www.
springframework.org/schema/beans/spring-beans-current.xsd">
    <amqp:connector name="localhostAMQPConnector"
activeDeclarationsOnly="true" doc:name="AMQP-0-9 Connector"/>

    <flow name="rabbitmq-sample-flow">
<amqp:inbound-endpoint responseTimeout="10000"
doc:name="rabbitmq-inbound-endpoint" queueName="test-queue"
queueDurable="true" connector-ref="localhostAMQPConnector"/>
<amqp:outbound-endpoint responseTimeout="10000"
doc:name="rabbitmq-outbound-endpoint"
queueName="test-destination-queue" routingKey="test-destination-queue"
queueDurable="true" connector-ref="localhostAMQPConnector"/>
</flow>
</mule>
```

In order to use the AMQP transport, you need to provide the Mule AMQP transport and RabbitMQ Java client on your classpath. The Maven dependency for the transport library is as follows:

```
<dependency>
    <groupId>org.mule.transports</groupId>
    <artifactId>mule-transport-amqp</artifactId>
    <version>3.3.0</version>
</dependency>
```

However, Anypoint studio can dynamically deploy the AMQP client and Mule AMQP transport dependencies to your Mule ESB at runtime, and so, you need to copy them manually to the runtime libraries in the following path:

```
<anypoint_install_path>\plugins\org.mule.tooling.server.<version>\
mule\lib\mule
```

If you are using version 3.4.1 of the Mule AMQP transport and version 3.2.1 of the client, copy `mule-transport-amqp-3.4.1.jar` and `amqp-client-3.2.1.jar` files from the local Maven repository to that directory. If you don't do this, you may get an error that states Mule ESB fails to find a namespace handler for the AMQP transport declarations in your Mule configuration.

Mule ESB uses byte array representation of messages, so if you want to convert the byte array into a string, you can either use a proper AMQP transformer and register it in the Mule runtime or convert the byte array manually in your application. To test your setup, you can send a test message to the **test-queue** queue using the `RabbitTemplateExample` class with that queue and bind a listener such as the one specified by the `ContainerListenerExample` class to **test-destination-queue**. However, the `handleMessage()` method should be refactored a little bit in order to accept a byte array as a message:

```
public void handleMessage(Object message) {
    System.out.println("Message received: " +
new String((byte[])message);
}
```

WSO2

WSO2 is an open source ESB that is used by a number of enterprises including eBay. It also provides integration with the AMQP protocol. There is also an Eclipse-based IDE for WSO2 (WSO2 Developer Studio) to develop WSO2 applications. Download the WSO2 distributable that contains the WSO2 ESB along with an administrative web interface and unzip it to a proper location. Navigate to the **bin** directory and execute the following command to start the WSO2 message broker (assuming that we are running a Windows OS):

```
wso2server.bat --run
```

After the server has successfully started, you should be able to open the administrative web from the `https://localhost:9443` URL and log in with the admin/admin default credentials. A screen similar to the following will be displayed:

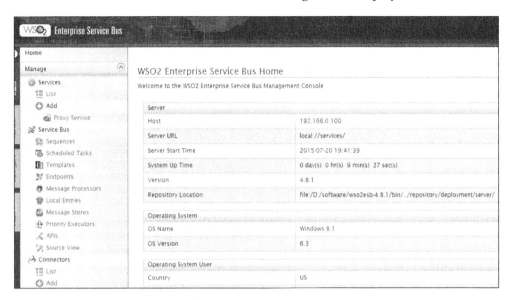

The WSO2 ESB steps on the WSO2 carbon platform, which is an OSGi-based middleware. The WSO2 carbon platform provides support for the provisioning of dependencies (OSGi bundles) from an Equinox p2 repository. The WSO2 RabbitMQ AMQP transport is also provided in a p2 repository that can be downloaded locally from the WSO2 website. After you download the p2 repository of the AMQP transport bundles and unzip it, navigate to **Configure -> Features** from the administrative interface and specify the path to the local repository along with a proper name from the repository, and click on **Add**. Then, specify the newly added repository, unselect **Group features by category**, click on **Find Features**, specify the **Axis2 Transport RabbitMQ AMQP** feature, click on the **Install** button, and follow the steps from the installation process. Add the following to the **listeners** configuration in `<wso2_install_path>/repository/conf/axis2/axis2.xml` in order to create a RabbitMQ transport listener for WSO2:

```
<transportReceiver name="rabbitmq"
class="org.apache.axis2.transport.rabbitmq.RabbitMQListener">
<parameter name="AMQPConnectionFactory" locked="false">
<parameter name="rabbitmq.server.host.name"
locked="false">localhost</parameter>
<parameter name="rabbitmq.server.port"
locked="false">5672</parameter>
<parameter name="rabbitmq.server.user.name"
locked="false">guest</parameter>
```

```
<parameter name="rabbitmq.server.password"
locked="false">guest</parameter>
</parameter>
</transportReceiver>
```

The **locked** attribute specifies that the parameters cannot be overridden by a WSO2 service. Add the following to configure the RabbitMQ transport sender in the `axis2.xml` configuration file:

```
<transportSender name="rabbitmq"
class="org.apache.axis2.transport.rabbitmq.RabbitMQSender"/>
```

Apart from this, the ESB runtime may not need to load the RabbitMQ transport libraries (even though they have been installed from the p2 repository), and so you may need to copy them from the p2 repository to the `<wso2_install_path>\repository\components\lib` directory. As the libraries might be a little outdated with regard to the version of RabbitMQ that you are using, you can also download the source code of the WSO2 transports from GitHub, build the Maven project for the RabbitMQ transport, and replace the old version in the preceding directory. You need to make sure that the version of the transport library works with your version of the RabbitMQ broker.

After you have installed the RabbitMQ AMQP transport and added the configuration for the sender and receiver, restart the WSO2 server in order to load the new feature along with the configured transports.

Now, we are ready to configure a proxy service that will allow us to transfer messages from **test-queue** to **test-destination-queue** using the WSO2 ESB.

First, create an endpoint that will be used by the RabbitMQ transport sender by navigating to **Main -> Endpoints -> Add Endpoint -> Address Endpoint**:

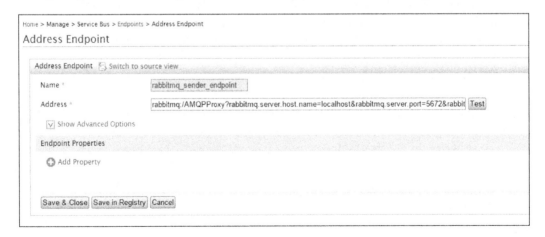

Specify the following settings:

- **Name**: `rabbitmq_sender_endpoint`

- **Address**: `rab-bitmq:/rabbitmq_proxy_service?rabbitmq.server.host.name=127.0.0.1 & rab-bitmq.server.port=5672 & rabbitmq.server.user.name=guest&rabbitmq.server.password=guest&rabbitmq.queue.name=test-destination-queue`

- Click on the **Save & Close** button. Click on the **Switch Off** link under the **Action** menu in order to enable the endpoint. The address uses the RabbitMQ transport that we defined in the Apache Axis2 configuration along with the `rabbitmq_proxy_service` proxy service that uses the specified RabbitMQ parameters to send a message to the `test-destination-queue` queue. The same `rabbitmq_proxy_service` service will be used to retrieve messages from the test-queue queue, and if the two queues are missing, they will be created from the RabbitMQ transport. Create the proxy service by clicking on **Add -> Proxy Service -> Custom Proxy**, and click on **Switch to Source View** in order to provide the service configuration without using the wizard:

```xml
<?xml version="1.0" encoding="UTF-8"?>
<proxy xmlns="http://ws.apache.org/ns/synapse"
       name="rabbitmq_proxy_service"
       transports="rabbitmq"
       statistics="disable"
       trace="disable"
       startOnLoad="true">
   <target endpoint="rabbitmq_sender_endpoint">
      <inSequence>
         <log level="full"/>
         <property name="OUT_ONLY" value="true"/>
         <property name="FORCE_SC_ACCEPTED" value="true"
scope="axis2"/>
      </inSequence>
   </target>
   <parameter name="rabbitmq.queue.name"> test-queue</parameter>
   <parameter name="rabbitmq.connection.factory">
AMQPConnectionFactory</parameter>
   <description/>
</proxy>
```

The proxy uses the RabbitMQ transport in order to subscribe to the test-queue queue using `AMQPConnectionFactory` to create an AMQP connection. The `inSequence` section specifies how a message received from the test-queue queue is processed. We enable full logging (that also prints the message in the WSO2 console) and we specify that we do not expect a response once we forward the message to an endpoint (using the `OUT_ONLY` attribute). `FORCE_SC_ACCEPTED` is used to indicate that the ESB must send an acknowledgement after the message was successfully received. We also provide a reference to the `rabbitmq_sender_endpoint` endpoint so that received messages are sent using the RabbitMQ transport sender to this endpoint. Click on the **Save** button in order to save and deploy the proxy service. In order to check whether your setup works fine, you can use the Java client library or Spring framework in order to send a message to the test-queue queue and subscribe to the test-destination-queue queue as shown earlier. As the WSO2 endpoint is exposed as an Apache Axis2 SOAP web service, you need to send a SOAP message to the RabbitMQ broker and additionally specify the content type as text/xml and content encoding as `utf-8` along with a `SOAP_ACTION` message header that specifies the SOAP action you are specifying in the message. The following snippet uses the Java client library in order to create an AMQP message in the proper format to be handled by the WSO2 proxy service:

```
String soapMessage = "<soapenv:Envelope " + "xmlns:soapenv=\"http://
schemas.xmlsoap.org/soap/envelope/\">\n" + <soapenv:Header/>\n" +
<soapenv:Body>\n" + <p:test xmlns:p=\"http://test.service.sample.
com\"> \n" +
<in>" + "sample message" + "</in>\n" +
</p:test>\n" + "</soapenv:Body>\n" + </soapenv:Envelope>";
BasicProperties.Builder props  = new BasicProperties.Builder();
props.contentType("text/xml");
props.contentEncoding("utf-8");

Map<String, Object> headers = new HashMap<String, Object>();
headers.put("SOAP_ACTION", "test");
props.headers(headers);
channel.basicPublish(DEFAULT_EXCHANGE, QUEUE_NAME,
props.build(), message.getBytes());
```

In case you don't want to format and parse SOAP messages as this can introduce unnecessary complexity in your integration scenario, then you can use the WSO2 message broker that handles AMQP messages and integrates with the WSO2 ESB via JMS.

Integration with databases

Most relational and NoSQL databases provide a built-in language to create programs directly at the database level. Whether this is PL/SQL or Java for the Oracle database, T/SQL for the MSSQL server, or JavaScript for MongoDB, most of them can leverage the use of the client utilities provided by RabbitMQ in order to establish a direct connection to the message broker and persist data from AMQP messages. In many cases, it might be easier and more proper to use a database API along with a RabbitMQ client library written in the same language via a proper application running outside the database. In this section, we will look at how to integrate the RabbitMQ broker with several widely used databases.

Oracle RDBMS

If you decide to use PL/SQL, you will have to supply your own PL/SQL AMQP client implementation, which can turn out to be a lot of work unless you manage to find a publicly available implementation. (At the time of writing this, no such free or commercial distribution is available.) As the Oracle database provides support for multiple languages, we can use Java stored procedures in the database. In order to create a publisher or subscriber as a stored procedure, we can use the following procedure:

- Load the RabbitMQ Java client library in the database
- Load the Java stored procedures to publish/subscribe (static Java methods)
- Define PL/SQL procedures that call the loaded Java stored procedures

We will use Oracle database 12c. The `loadjava` command-line utility supplied by the Oracle database allows us to load Java classes, source files, or resource files in a database schema. We can use the utility to load the RabbitMQ Java client library along with the additional required libraries using the utility as follows (assuming that we are retrieving the libraries from the local Maven repository in a Windows operating system):

```
cd %userprofile%/.m2
loadjava -u c##demo -resolve -resolver "((* C##DEMO) (* PUBLIC))"
repository\log4j\log4j\1.2.16\log4j-1.2.16.jar
loadjava -u c##demo -resolve -resolver "((* C##DEMO) (* PUBLIC))"
repository\commons-logging\commons-logging\1.2\commons-logging-1.2.jar
loadjava -u c##demo -resolve -resolver "((* C##DEMO) (* PUBLIC))"
repository\org\slf4j\slf4j-api\1.6.1\slf4j-api-1.6.1.jar
loadjava -u c##demo -resolve -resolver "((* C##DEMO) (* PUBLIC))"
repository\org\slf4j\slf4j-log4j12\1.6.1\slf4j-log4j12-1.6.1.jar
loadjava -u c##demo -resolve -resolver "((* C##DEMO) (* PUBLIC))"
repository\com\rabbitmq\amqp-client\3.4.1\amqp-client-3.4.1.jar
```

We used the `resolve` option in order to try resolving the loaded Java classes from the specified JAR files. In case there is a resolution failure, a console output will provide information on the resolution error. In case there are missing classes during the loading of libraries, you must find and load the libraries that contain these classes first. We are also specifying `resolver`, which serves as `CLASSPATH` to resolve dependencies from database schemas. In this particular case, we are using the `C##DEMO` user schema and the `PUBLIC` schema, which contains the core Java classes.

Navigate to the directory of your compiled Java classes created in *Chapter 2, Design Patterns with RabbitMQ*, and load them using the `loadjava` utility:

```
loadjava -u c##demo -resolve -resolver "((* C##DEMO) (* PUBLIC))"
Sender.class
loadjava -u c##demo -resolve -resolver "((* C##DEMO) (* PUBLIC))"
DefaultExchangeSenderDemo.class
loadjava -u c##demo -resolve -resolver "((* C##DEMO) (* PUBLIC))"
CompetingReceiver.class
loadjava -u c##demo -resolve -resolver "((* C##DEMO) (* PUBLIC))"
CompetingReceiverDemo*.class
```

Note the `*` operator after the name of the `CompetingReceiverDemo` class. This will also load the inner classes defined in the `CompetingReceiverDemo` class.

Now, you can bind the static methods from the sender and receiver demo classes to the PL/SQL stored procedures using a tool such as SQL*Plus or SQLDeveloper:

```
CREATE OT REPLACE PROCEDURE RABBITMQ_SENDER AS
 LANGUAGE JAVA NAME 'org.packt.rabbitmq.book.samples.chapter2.
DefaultExchangeSenderDemo.sendToDefaultExchange()';

CREATE OT REPLACE PROCEDURE RABBITMQ_RECEIVER AS
 LANGUAGE JAVA NAME 'org.packt.rabbitmq.book.samples.chapter2.
CompetingReceiverDemo.main(java.lang.String[])';
```

To test the stored procedures, you can first enable `DBMS_OUTPUT`. In SQLDeveloper, you can do this from the Dbms Output view or use the `SET SERVEROUTPUT ON` command in SQL*Plus. In order to enable the mapping of `System.out` and logger output to `DBMS_OUTPUT`, invoke the `set_output()` stored procedure with a buffer size of 2,000 bytes as follows:

```
EXECUTE DBMS_JAVA.SET_OUTPUT(2000);
```

To test your RabbitMQ sender stored procedure, execute the following:

```
EXECUTE RABBITMQ_SENDER;
```

To test your RabbitMQ receiver stored procedure, execute the following and send some test messages to the `event_queue` queue used by the sender and receiver:

```
EXECUTE RABBITMQ_RECEIVER;
```

You can observe the loaded Java classes from the current user schema using the following query:

```
SELECT * FROM USER_OBJECTS WHERE object_type LIKE '%JAVA%';
```

In case any of the loaded Java classes fails to resolve (in case we were not using the `resolve` option with the `loadjava` utility), then our class would be marked as `INVALID` in the **Status** column. If this happens, you can try to reload the proper libraries by first dropping them (using the `dropjava` utility with the same parameters) and then loading them again using the `loadjava` utility.

MongoDB

MongoDB is a document store that stores data hierarchically in a JSON format (compiled by the database to a binary JSON format called BSON). MongoDB is used in a variety of scenarios where performance and eventual consistency are favored with regard to the transactional consistency provided by relational databases such as Oracle. In order to integrate RabbitMQ with MongoDB, it may be more appropriate to use the NodeJS MongoDB driver along with a NodeJS AMQP client implementation to establish the integration using server-side JavaScript or creating a Java application that uses the MongoDB Java driver along with the RabbitMQ Java library either directly or via the Spring framework (using Spring Data for MongoDB and Spring AMQP for RabbitMQ).

Hadoop

To integrate with a Hadoop cluster, you can use a Java application that serves as a mediator between the Hadoop cluster and RabbitMQ instance/cluster. Another option is to use the Apache Flume project, which provides a mechanism to aggregate data from multiple sources in a Hadoop database. Apache Flume has an AMQP plugin that can be used to create a RabbitMQ source from which to retrieve data for further processing and storage in a Hadoop cluster.

RabbitMQ integrations

RabbitMQ provides adapters for various other types of protocol in the form of RabbitMQ plugins. Such protocols include STOMP, MQTT, HTTP, Websocket, and others. Each adapter plugin follows a common usage pattern:

- The login information is passed in terms of the capabilities provided by the particular protocol to the RabbitMQ broker for authentication

- SSL support is provided for most of the protocol adapter plugins

- Adapter plugins expose TCP ports on which they accept the connection via the protocol that they implement, for example, by default, the STOMP adapter is configured to use 61613 (TCP) and 61614 (SSL), and for MQTT, these are 1883 (TCP) and 8883 (SSL)

- Adapter plugins use a particular syntax to specify the RabbitMQ endpoint elements such as exchanges, queues, and bindings that are used when protocol messages are translated to particular operations on the broker (such as subscriptions on the sending of messages to the broker)

You can install protocol adapter plugins with the `rabbitmq_plugins` utility. For example, the `STOMP` plugin comes with the RabbitMQ broker installation and must be enabled with the following command:

```
rabbitmq-plugins.bat enable rabbitmq-stomp
```

In case you want to use RabbitMQ directly from the browser using Websockets, you can additionally install the `rabbitmq-web-stomp` plugin, which is a bridge between a SockJS Websocket server and the `rabbitmq-stomp` plugin to communicate with the broker via Websockets. There is also a separate plugin called `rabbitmq-web-stomp-examples` that demonstrates the use of `rabbitmq-web-stomp` using a web browser.

RabbitMQ deployment options

So far, we have been manually configuring our RabbitMQ instances. However, it's common for many production systems to use automatic provisioning and management of the configuration of components, including the message broker. There are a number of ways in which we can deploy and manage a RabbitMQ broker instance:

- Installing and configuring the broker manually in a virtual machine that is used to distribute it

- Automatically provisioning in a virtual container hosted directly on the operating system using a tool such as Docker, which provides integration with RabbitMQ

- Deploying or using managed RabbitMQ instances in the cloud; many platform-as-a-service cloud providers enable the use of such instances in the form of messaging-as-a-service or RabbitMQ-as-a-service (such as the Google Cloud and CloudAMQP platforms)

- Automatically provisioning a target operating system using a recipe written in a domain-specific language with a provisioning tool such as Puppet or Chef (both of them provide integration with RabbitMQ with some limitations with regard to the target operating systems)

- Using a combination of the preceding points; automatically creating a VirtualBox (or other) virtual machine or virtual container using Docker, and automatically provisioning the RabbitMQ instances along with their configurations using Puppet or Chef — this can be achieved with a tool such as Vagrant

In this section, we will look at some of the most widely used tools that allow us to deploy and configure the message broker using any of the preceding mechanisms.

Puppet

Download the open source version of the Puppet tool for your operating system (we will be using the one for Windows) from the Puppetlabs site and install it:

```
puppet module install puppetlabs-rabbitmq
```

After you install Puppet, you can install the RabbitMQ module using the following command. Note that the RabbitMQ Puppet plugin does not support a Windows-based configuration at the time of writing this book; you can try it with a Debian-based distribution such as RedHat or supply your own Puppet class that does the provisioning on Windows.

Create a file named `rabbitmq.pp` with the following contents that specifies the configuration of your RabbitMQ instance:

```
class { 'rabbitmq':
    port => '5666',
    service_manage => true,
    environment_variables => {
        'RABBITMQ_NODENAME' => 'RabbitMQ_Puppet',
        'RABBITMQ_SERVICENAME' => 'RabbitMQ_Puppet'
    }
}
```

To provision the instance on the same local machine, use the following command:

```
puppet apply rabbitmq.pp
```

Note that in a production scenario, you will typically use a master/client Puppet setup rather than local provisioning.

Docker

A Docker file contains the instructions to build a docker image. A RabbitMQ broker instance is started in a separate process running from a Docker image. The image runs the RabbitMQ instance in a Docker container. As Docker contains Linux-specific commands, you must run the image in a Linux environment (for example, Ubuntu). The steps required in order to run the image are as follows:

- Download and install Docker. If you are using Ubuntu, you can install it using the following command:

```
wget -qO- https://get.docker.com/ | sh
```

- Download and build the Docker Ubuntu container, and then download and build the RabbitMQ Docker image from the Docker Hub repository using the following commands:

```
sudo docker build -t="dockerfile/ubuntu" github.com/dockerfile/
ubuntu
sudo docker build -t="dockerfile/rabbitmq" github.com/dockerfile/
rabbitmq
```

- Run the RabbitMQ server from the image using the following command:

```
sudo docker run -d -p 5672:5672 -p 15672:15672 dockerfile/rabbitmq
```

The –p argument specifies port redirection. In the preceding case, RabbitMQ ports 5672 and 15672 from the docker image are mapped to ports 5672 and 15672 from the host machine. The steps defined in the RabbitMQ image are as follows:

1. Specify the Ubuntu Docker container that will run the RabbitMQ message broker.
2. Install the RabbitMQ message broker.
3. Enable the management plugin.
4. Define /data/mnesia and /data/log as the directories for the RabbitMQ database and log files.
5. Start the RabbitMQ broker instance.
6. Expose the RabbitMQ broker instance and management plugin ports (5672 and 15672) from the container.

Vagrant

In case you decide to create a VirtualBox VM with RabbitMQ using a Vagrant script, then perform the following steps:

1. Download and install Vagrant.

2. Download and install VirtualBox.

3. Create a puppet file that provisions the RabbitMQ message broker and enables the management plugin.

4. Create a Vagrantfile that creates the VirtualBox VM and runs the Puppet script.

5. Fire up the VM using the following command:

   ```
   vagrant up
   ```

Testing RabbitMQ applications

Testing is essential to ensure that a system works as expected. In this sense, the message broker is no exception. In the next sections, we will cover very briefly the different aspects of testing applications that use RabbitMQ as a message broker.

Unit testing of RabbitMQ applications

You can test applications that publish/subscribe to a RabbitMQ broker by isolating client API calls to the broker using a mocking framework such as JMock or Mockito in case of Java. The mocking library to use depends on the language that you are using to interact with the broker, but, in general, you would mock calls to the broker as you would with any other type of external system that is used by your application.

Integration testing of RabbitMQ applications

In case you are using only AMQP 0-9-1 features in your communication with the RabbitMQ broker, you can use an embedded AMQP server. Apache Qpid provides an embedded version that you can use in your integration tests. In order to use it, you can include the following Maven dependency:

```
<dependency>
    <groupId>org.apache.qpid</groupId>
    <artifactId>qpid-broker</artifactId>
    <version>0.14</version>
    <scope>test</scope>
</dependency>
```

In order to create, configure, and start a Qpid broker instance, you can use the following code:

```
BrokerOptions configuration = new BrokerOptions("config.json");
Broker broker = new Broker();
broker.startup(configuration);
```

The `config.json` file specifies the Qpid configuration. After you start the AMQP server, you can use a proper test configuration to redirect your AMQP client communication to the embedded AMQP server in your test framework. In case you are using RabbitMQ-specific extensions such as publisher confirms, you may want to start up RabbitMQ as an external process in your test suite.

Case study: Integrating CSN with external systems

As the workload of CSN continued to increase and the CSN team expanded as well, a number of new enhancements to the system were introduced:

- The CSN web and worker nodes were refactored to use Spring AMQP instead of the Java client library for communication with the broker, which improved maintenance of the nodes.

- The browser plugin used to accept chat messages was removed in favor of SockJS websockets used along with the newly provisioned rabbitmq-web-stomp plugin. This further improved the maintenance of the system.

- A separate application was used to store data from the broker to the Oracle database, but it was decommissioned in favor of the Java stored procedures used to retrieve messages from the broker for the purposes of backup.

- More integration tests to test the communication with the message broker were introduced as part of the system building.

- Puppet scripts to deploy the separate components of the system, including the RabbitMQ broker, were created.

Summary

In this chapter, we covered a lot of areas related to the integration of the RabbitMQ message broker with other types of system. The Spring AMQP and Spring integration frameworks were introduced as layers of abstraction on top of the RabbitMQ Java client libraries. Demonstrations on the use of RabbitMQ with the Mule and WSO2 ESBs were introduced following the pattern that we implemented using the Spring integration framework. We discussed how to integrate different types of database directly with the message broker and what types of adapter for other protocols the RabbitMQ broker provides. In the end, we saw how different provisioning tools provide support for RabbitMQ so that it can be deployed in a purely automated manner and how to test applications using the broker.

Exercises

1. How does the Spring framework integrate with RabbitMQ?

2. How does RabbitMQ integrate with the Mule and WSO2 ESBs?

3. How can you create an Oracle stored procedure to publish/subscribe to a RabbitMQ broker?

4. How does RabbitMQ provide support with other messaging protocols?

5. How can you provide integration of RabbitMQ with MySQL and Cassandra?

6. What deployment options do you have for RabbitMQ?

7. How can you test applications that communicate with a RabbitMQ message broker?

7
Performance Tuning and Monitoring

Performance is a critical requirement for many applications. Each component in the communication flow between the components in a system impacts performance, including the message broker. In this chapter, we will focus our attention on optimizing and monitoring the performance of the RabbitMQ message broker and using various benchmarks to compare RabbitMQ against other brokers.

The following topics will be covered in this chapter:

- Performance tuning of RabbitMQ instances
- Monitoring RabbitMQ instances
- Comparing RabbitMQ with other message brokers

Performance tuning of RabbitMQ instances

Tuning the performance of a system is, in many cases, a nontrivial process that is conducted gradually over time. This also applies to the message broker itself. The RabbitMQ team has done a pretty good job in optimizing the various bits and pieces of the broker over time. One such example is topic exchanges. Version 2.4.0 significantly improved the performance of message routing from topic exchanges using a tire data structure. Another one is the significant improvement in performance predictability in version 2.8.1 during the heavy loading of the message broker due to improved memory management. However, there are many scenarios that require the tuning of the broker based on the usage patterns and properties of the system, as we shall see in this chapter.

To understand better how to tune the performance of our broker, let's take a look at the standard three-tier broker setup:

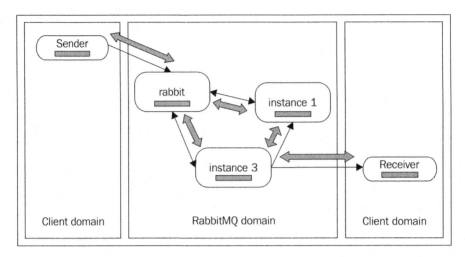

We can consider performance tuning at each level of message passing as follows:

- The sender may decide to optimize the way it establishes the connection to the broker (the number of channels created, usage of multiple threads for the creation of channels, and sending of messages), the size of the messages (whether the compression or batching of messages is proper), whether to use AMQP transactions or publisher confirms (which may hit message performance in terms of reliable delivery—reliability typically always implies a trade-off for performance), and message TTL (time to live).

- The network link between the sender/consumer and broker might be an issue. While in systems where RabbitMQ is a component that provides loosely-coupled communication between the system components running on the same server or server cluster, network links may not be an issue, but if we use RabbitMQ to process messages being sent from a system on a remote network, this may be an issue. In this case, it is a shared responsibility between the AMQP client and server to tune the way channels are created in a connection or the size of messages processed in the channel. One possible solution would be to establish a dedicated line between the sender/consumer and broker. Network tuning may improve the communication link; network optimizations are out of scope for this chapter.

- Broker optimizations are for focus points when we discuss performance tuning in terms of RabbitMQ. This involves a number of aspects such as memory management, CPU utilization (in terms of multiple cores), storage of persistent and transient messages on the disk, faster execution of Erlang code from the RabbitMQ broker, impact of node synchronization and queue mirroring in a cluster, per queue message TTL customization, queue creation/deletion rates, message sending/consumption rates, and complexity of binding key patterns.

- The consumer may use similar optimization techniques as the sender with the addition of broker subscription management (such as preventing excessive subscriptions to the broker).

To check the performance load, you need to prepare a maximum-sized volume of messages of the expected size to send for the processing and measuring of latency and throughput. Let's kick off our performance tuning guide by taking into account these considerations.

Memory usage

Persistent messages are always written to the disk once they arrive on a queue, while transient messages will be written to the disk under high memory consumption (based on the memory limit specified for use by the RabbitMQ broker instance). Each disk operation slows down the message processing. By default, RabbitMQ is configured to use up to 40% of the physical RAM on the machine on which an instance runs; although this is not guaranteed as it only implies a threshold at which publishers are notified to slow down message sending (throttled). Be careful to set the parameter properly in case multiple RabbitMQ instances are running on the same physical/virtual machine. Assuming that you have a single instance running per workstation, you can increase the parameter so that RabbitMQ may consume more memory for its queues. This can be done either in the RabbitMQ configuration file or using the `rabbitmqctl` utility as follows:

```
rabbitmqctl set_vm_memory_high_watermark 0.7
```

You should see a message that tells you whether the memory threshold has been set successfully:

```
Setting memory threshold on rabbit@DOMAIN to 0.7 ...
```

In this case, we are assuming that a single instance is running on the workstation and there are no other applications running on the same server. In case you run a cluster of three nodes on the same machine, you may want to set the parameter to each of them to something less than 0.33 (for example, 0.25):

```
rabbitmqctl set_vm_memory_high_watermark 0.25
rabbitmqctl -n instance1 set_vm_memory_high_watermark 0.25
rabbitmqctl -n instance2 set_vm_memory_high_watermark 0.25
```

Before RabbitMQ hits the memory limit in order to start the persistence of messages on the disk (persistent messages are already stored on the disk as they are persisted upon arrival in the queue, but they need to be removed from memory anyway), saving to the disk starts earlier (by default, when 50% of the maximum memory limit is reached). To change this threshold (let's say, to 80%), you need to set the vm_memory_high_watermark_paging_ratio parameter per each RabbitMQ node as follows:

```
rabbitmqctl eval "application:set_env
(rabbit, vm_memory_high_watermark_paging_ratio, 0.8). "
```

You can also set the parameter in the RabbitMQ configuration file before the node is started. The memory consumption in the broker is affected by the number of client connections, number of queues and messages in each of them, enabled plugins and the amount of memory that they use, in-memory Mnesia metadata and message store index, and the additional amount of memory used by the Erlang VM.

Faster runtime execution

Erlang supports the **HiPE** (**High Performance Erlang**) compilation for some platforms that improves the performance of message processing by the RabbitMQ broker. (At the time of writing, this was still in the experimental phase.) The HiPe compiler is pretty similar in comparison to a server Java virtual machine — more native optimizations are done on the startup of the server Java application resulting in an improved runtime execution. In many scenarios, the start up time of the RabbitMQ broker may not be critical so HiPe compilation may be a good optimization. Behind the scenes, the Erlang VM precompiles the RabbitMQ modules by passing the [native] parameter to the compiler that triggers the HiPE compilation. On some platforms, however (such as Windows at the time of writing), the HiPE compilation is not supported. In order to enable the HiPE compilation for RabbitMQ, you can set the hipe_compile parameter to true in the RabbitMQ configuration file. In case the HiPE compilation is not enabled for the particular platform where the RabbitMQ instances are running, you will get a message in the instance logs that the HiPE compilation is not performed.

Message size

Smaller messages can improve the latency (time to process a single message) and throughput (message rate per period of time). To reduce the message size, you can use a proper format for the marshalling and unmarshalling of messages, for example, JSON instead of XML. Try to avoid additional information as part of the message in order to reduce the size of the message further.

The maximum frame size of messages

A frame is a basic unit of data transfer in the AMQP protocol. There are different types of AMQP frames used to establish the AMQP protocol life cycle. The transfer frame is particularly used to transfer the message data between the RabbitMQ broker and clients. The size of the message frame can affect the latency and throughout. Typically, this value should not be changed but in case you have messages bigger than 128 MB (the default maximum frame size), then message fragmentation occurs—the message is split into multiple frames. The more fragmentation there is, the less throughout there is for the messages. The minimum size of frames in RabbitMQ is 4 KB. Although the smaller maximum size of frames may degrade the throughput, it may improve the latency, but you need to measure the performance of your setup. To change the maximum frame size, you can set the `frame_max` parameter to a particular value (in bytes) in the RabbitMQ configuration file.

The maximum number of channels

The number of channels created from a connection to the RabbitMQ server can affect the performance. An application can achieve better throughput if more channels are used, and the application uses a channel-per-thread approach to send messages. However, the more channels there are in the RabbitMQ message broker, the more memory is consumed. To set the maximum number of channels that an application can use, use the `channel_max` parameter in the RabbitMQ configuration file. The default value is zero meaning that there is no limit for the number of channels that an application can create.

Connection heartbeats

Connection heartbeats provide a mechanism to detect a dead TCP connection from the client (sender/consumer) and RabbitMQ broker. The mechanism works by setting a heartbeat timeout from the RabbitMQ client. (By default, it is set to 580 seconds, which can be a pretty big timeout depending on your messaging use cases.) The RabbitMQ server sends a heartbeat frame to the client and waits for a response. If either side of the connection detects that more than two heartbeats have been missed, then a TCP connection is detected that can be typically handled by the client by catching a proper exception (`MissedHeartbeatException` is thrown by the RabbitMQ Java client). A heartbeat is sent every timeout/2 period of time. The heartbeat timeout can be changed by either setting the heartbeat parameter in the RabbitMQ configuration file or using a proper method in the RabbitMQ client library to set a value for the heartbeat period before creating a connection to the broker. Make sure that the heartbeat is set to at least a few seconds as the performance can degrade (especially in cases when the broker performs intense message processing).

Clustering and high availability

Clustering can affect the performance of the broker in terms of several different aspects. Heartbeats cannot be sent only between the clients and RabbitMQ broker but also between nodes in a RabbitMQ cluster in order to detect node availability. The `net_ticktime` parameter specifies the frequency of sending heartbeat messages between nodes in the cluster. The default value is 60 seconds, which means that a heartbeat is being sent roughly every 15 seconds (four times per `net_ticktime` period). Decreasing this value to just a few seconds in a large cluster can have a slight effect on the performance of the cluster. This applies to `cluster_keepalive_interval` that is used to send keepalive messages from a node to all the other nodes in the cluster and indicates that the node is up (the default is 10,000 milliseconds). A much larger value than 60 seconds imposes a risk of detecting a dead node too late in time.

Another factor could be the rate of exchange/queue creation and deletion in a cluster. As every queue creates a new Erlang process and the information about the queue must be synchronized with all the nodes in the cluster, this can consume additional resources and decrease the performance. Imagine that you have a large number of queues and exchanges being created in a cluster, each one of them creates a separate Erlang process on the cluster node on which it is created, and information about each queue must propagate to each node in the cluster using Erlang message passing. Each cluster node needs to persist the information about the exchanges, queues, and other items in the cluster on the disk (depending on the type of node). Now, imagine that you have a large cluster and each queue being created/deleted is mirrored over all the nodes in the cluster, then you have a recipe for performance issues.

The following is a short list of guidelines considering the performance in terms of clustering and high availability:

- Try to minimize the number of exchanges and queues created and deleted in a RabbitMQ cluster.

- If you have a large enough number of disk nodes and you want to scale, you can add RAM nodes instead of DISK nodes in order to improve the performance in terms of exchange/queue creation.

- Mirror a queue on several other nodes in the cluster rather than all the nodes in the cluster. The replication factor depends on your reliability constraints, but replicating the queue contents over all the nodes in the cluster can hit the performance seriously, especially when you have a large RabbitMQ cluster.

- Choose carefully which queues need to be mirrored and avoid the mirroring of queues that need to imply message reliability.

- Last but not least, try to distribute the queues evenly among the nodes in a cluster.

QoS prefetching

If you have been sending messages to a queue and one or a few consumers subscribe to this queue, the consumers may try to fetch and buffer a large number of messages for consumption before sending any acknowledgments, which can actually drain resources on the consumer node and slow it down. To prevent this, you can use the `basic.qos` operation during the channel creation (when creating the channel from the client) to specify the maximum number of messages that can be prefetched (buffered) by a consumer before they are acknowledged. For example, using the Java client, you can set the prefetch count to 50 per channel consumer using the following line of code:

```
channel.basicQos(50);
```

A channel can have a prefetch count limit regardless of the number of consumers:

```
channel.basicQos(100, true);
```

The general recommendation is to set a higher prefetch count (for example, 40 or 50) in order to improve the performance. However, a large prefetch count can prevent the event distribution of messages among the consumers and so the value must be tuned with caution.

Message persistence

Message persistence in RabbitMQ also affects the processing time for messages. We already discussed that transient and persistent messages need to be persisted on the disk by RabbitMQ. The persistence layer in RabbitMQ provides a message store to store messages on the disk and also a queue index to keep information about the location of a message in a queue and additional information (for example, whether the message has been acknowledged or not) in memory. When under memory pressure, the queue index may still preserve small messages in-memory and flush only large messages to the message store. The default size of messages that RabbitMQ tries to keep in-memory is 4 kilobytes and is specified by the `queue_index_embed_msgs_below` parameter, which can be modified in the RabbitMQ configuration file. Setting a larger value of the parameter can allow you to store more messages in-memory, thus reducing IO operations. However, as each queue index points to a segment file held in-memory that can store 16, 384, increasing the value of the `queue_index_embed_msgs_below` parameter even slightly may increase the memory consumption drastically on the broker with regard to improved performance. Another way that the performance might be affected based on your scenario would be using a custom backing store that allows you to store messages in a manner different from the default backing store that writes them to the disk. This can either improve or decrease the performance of your message broker. In *Chapter 10, Internals* we will demonstrate how to write a RabbitMQ plugin that uses a custom database as a message store for RabbitMQ.

For more information about message persistence and backing stores used in RabbitMQ, you can review the following posts from the RabbitMQ documentation:

- Check this link for persistence configuration: `https://www.rabbitmq.com/persistence-conf.html`

- RabbitMQ backing stores: `http://www.rabbitmq.com/blog/2011/01/20/rabbitmq-backing-stores-databases-and-disks/`

Mnesia transaction logs

The Mnesia database used by RabbitMQ supports the atomicity of operations via transactions. Each transaction log is stored in the memory before being flushed to the disk (in the database itself) and this is performed periodically by Mnesia. This can affect the performance due to the number of disk writes. To reduce disk writes, you can increase the size of the transaction log entries kept by Mnesia in-memory by setting the `dump_log_write_threshold` parameter in the configuration file (default value is 100).

Acknowledgements, transactions and publisher confirms

In case you release the reliability constraints, you can improve the performance by avoiding the usage of message acknowledgements, AMQP transactions, and publisher confirms. In case this is not acceptable, you can at least release some constraints. For publishers, you can use publisher confirms for a batch of messages. For consumers, you can send a single acknowledgment (using the `basic.ack` AMQL command) for multiple messages by specifying a multiple flag set to `true` and `delivery_tag` set to `0` rather than sending an acknowledgement for each message separately. Prefer publisher confirms instead of AMQP transactions for much better performance.

Message routing

The performance can be hit not only by the complexity of the binding key, but also by the type of exchange that you use. Topic exchanges are slower than direct or fanout exchanges, and a headers exchange can be slower than a direct exchange that is dependent on the number of message keys used to determine where a message will be routed by the headers exchange. A headers exchange can be slower than a topic exchange. In case both types of exchanges are an option for your messaging scenario, make sure that you measure the performance using both types of exchanges.

Queue creation/deletion

We already discussed that queue creation and deletion might be one of the factors that affects the performance in terms of synchronization between nodes in a cluster. There are other queue parameters that can affect the performance (both running a single node and cluster). Queues can be created with the `auto-delete` flag set to true. For example, using the Java client and an already created channel, you can declare `sample_queue` as `auto-delete`:

```
channel.queueDeclare("sample_queue", false, false, true, null);
```

If the queue does not have any consumers, it is never deleted. However, after the already existing subscribers are removed (either unsubscribed from the queue or dropped due to a connection failure), then the queue is automatically deleted and must be created again. If you have a large number of such queues, then intensive queue creation and deletion can affect message processing. You can also achieve the same effect by setting a rather small value for the queue **TTL** (**Time-to-live**), fro example, just a few milliseconds. In this case, after there are no consumers and no operations to retrieve a message from the queue have been performed for the specified TTL period of time, then the queue is dropped. The following example sets a TTL of just five milliseconds on the `sample_queue` queue when it is declared using the `x-expires` parameter. Note that you can set it as a policy for all the queues using the `rabbitmqctl` utility as well; refer to the RabbitMQ documentation.

```
Map<String, Object> args = new HashMap<String, Object>();
args.put("x-expires", 5).
channel.queueDeclare("sample_queue", false, false, false, args)
```

Queue message TTL

In order to avoid the saturation of a queue, which can slow down the processing of subsequent messages and increase the risk of overconsumption when one or more consumers are present as we already saw in QoS prefetching, we can set a per-queue message TTL. The following example sets a message TTL for the `sample_queue` queue using the `x-message-ttl` parameter set to two minutes:

```
Map<String, Object> args = new HashMap<String, Object>();
args.put("x-message-ttl", 120000).
channel.queueDeclare("sample_queue", false, false, false, args);
```

You can also set a per-message TTL but this will not solve the problem with queue saturation as messages stay in the queue even after their TTL has expired and are dropped when they reach the top of the queue (just before being consumed).

Alarms

Alarms are triggered by the RabbitMQ broker when memory or disk size limits are exceeded. We already saw how to configure memory usage using `set_vm_memory_high_watermark`. This parameter also specifies when producer throttling (intentional slowing down of message sending) takes place. Producer connection can also be blocked entirely in case a memory goes critically high; the management UI shows this condition in the **Connections** tab for the blocked connections. Disk size can also be an issue for the performance. By default, RabbitMQ requires at least 50 MB of free disk space on the location of the RabbitMQ message store. If this threshold is hit, the throttling of the producers and connection blocking starts taking place. A general recommendation from the RabbitMQ documentation is to set the minimum free disk size to the amount of memory installed on the machine. To do this, you can set the `disk_free_limit` parameter in the RabbitMQ configuration file. You can also set a value relative to the amount of memory on the machine by setting `disk_free_limit` to `{mem_relative, 1.0}`. You should, however, check the RabbitMQ log files on the particular node to make sure that RabbitMQ has managed to detect the size of the memory on the machine properly. For example, on an 8 GB machine with a default setting of 40% for the maximum memory limit for use by the broker, you can see something similar to the following:

```
Memory limit set to 3241MB of 8104MB total.
```

You can also use the `rabbitmqctl` utility to check the current setting of the `disk_free_limit` and `set_vm_memory_high_watermark` parameters:

```
rabbitmqctl status
```

This outputs a lot of additional information such as the number of used file descriptors, used Erlang processes, and so on:

```
{vm_memory_high_watermark,0.4},
 {vm_memory_limit,3399178649},
 {disk_free_limit,50000000},
 {disk_free,87735959552},
 {file_descriptors,
     [{total_limit,8092},{total_used,4},{sockets_limit,7280},
{sockets_used,2}]},{processes,[{limit,1048576},{used,201}]},
```

If a memory or disk alarm has been raised, this will be displayed as part of the preceding output; if no alarms have been triggered, the parameter is an empty list:

```
{alarms,[]}
```

Now, you can see that when a memory or disk alarm triggers, the performance can slow down drastically. So, apart from a decent amount of memory and large enough limit of maximum memory for use by the broker, you also need a decent amount of disk space to store transient and persistent messages along with a proper setting of the minimum disk free space threshold taken into consideration by the message broker.

Network tuning

The RabbitMQ documentation mentions several network improvements that can increase the message throughput with the most significant one being the TCP buffer size. The operating system typically allocates memory automatically for a TCP connection buffer, but you can explicitly specify the size of the TCP buffer used by RabbitMQ connections using the RabbitMQ configuration. Another factor is Nagle's algorithm that provides you with more efficient handling of really small TCP packets. However, the algorithm can typically be disabled in case you don't send small-sized TCP packets as this can even decrease the performance. The following configuration of the `tcp_listen_options` parameter in the RabbitMQ configuration sets the TCP buffers for the publisher/consumer connections to 256 KB and disables the Nagle's algorithm explicitly (it is disabled by default in the later versions of RabbitMQ clients but can be enabled when creating a connection from the client). For example, `ConnectionFactory` in the Java client uses a `SocketConfigurator` instance to configure the TCP socket to connect to the broker and disables the algorithm by default on the socket with `socket.setTcpNoDelay(true)`:

```
{nodelay,   true}
{sndbuf,    262144},
{recbuf,    262144}
```

In case you have a large number of connections, you can set this value to a smaller value and also increase the number of file handles used by the RabbitMQ instance. To do this, you can use the `ulimit` command in Linux before starting up your Rabbit instance. The following example sets the maximum open files handle to `65536`:

```
ulimit -n 65536
```

Another tuning option suggested by the RabbitMQ documentation is the size of the Erlang thread pool used to handle IO operations. A general recommendation is to use at least 12 threads per core. To set a value, you can set the following environment variable prior to starting the broker (in this example, we set the value to 96 for an eight-core machine):

```
RABBITMQ_SERVER_ADDITIONAL_ERL_ARGS="+A 96"
```

However, you don't have any guarantees that increasing the value will improve the throughput; you need to do the proper measurements.

Client tuning

You can improve the publisher/consumer performance in terms of message publishing or message consumption using more threads to create channels to the message broker. In terms of consumers, you must be careful when you share a channel among multiple threads (each using a separate set of queues) and you have QoS enabled for the shared channels. This can introduce unpredictable behavior among the consumers. Another case is when you have multiple subscriptions from different threads and you need to acknowledge multiple messages at once, this requires proper coordination among consumer threads, which will increase the complexity of your consumer.

Performance testing

We already discussed a variety of tuning options and we can use this knowledge to create a proper strategy for the performance tuning of our RabbitMQ instance/cluster. The process can be divided roughly into two phases executed iteratively:

- Perform a RabbitMQ optimization as suggested in the previous sections, such as changing a configuration parameter, policy, or a routing pattern, reducing the message size, or increasing system resources such as RAM or disk space (along with tuning of the proper RabbitMQ parameters).

- Measure the performance of your broker's setup and see if the performance improves. Always consider conducting performance tests on the maximum performance limits in non-peak hours even with the risk of crashing your system.

An ideal scenario would be if you have a test environment that mimics your production environment as closely as possible, and you can measure the performance over this setup and apply settings to the real environment without disrupting users or, even better, have a load balancer that would allow you to measure and tune the performance on only one node/cluster while the other nodes/clusters continue to operate normally. Unfortunately, this is not always the case, so you may need to do performance measurements and load testing directly on your production environment—better finding a bottleneck sooner than discovering it later the hard way. When conducting performance testing, you can consider the following basic factors and do proper combinations on any of them (based on your use cases):

- The size of messages
- The number of messages
- The type of messages (transient/persistent)

- The number of connections
- The number of channels
- The number of producers and consumers
- The ratio of the number of producers and consumers
- The number of pre-existing messages in a queue or set of queues

Typically, you try to use a tool that suits your own needs in terms of performance testing or use an already existing one. We will first briefly cover the PerfTest Java utility that comes with the RabbitMQ Java client and see how to use it in order to conduct performance measurements of our RabbitMQ message broker setup. Then, we will see how to build our own tool on top of PerfTest in order to execute performance tests against our current message broker setup in a loosely coupled manner (independent of the message broker implementation) and see later how to extend this tool with support for additional message brokers.

You can download the RabbitMQ Java client by cloning the `rabbitmq-codegen` and `rabbitmq-java-client` GitHub repository. You also need to install Python 2.x and the latest version of Ant in order to build the Java client (Python 3.x is not supported at the time of writing this book). To download and build the project after you have installed Python and Ant, execute the following:

```
git clone https://github.com/rabbitmq/rabbitmq-codegen
git clone https://github.com/rabbitmq/rabbitmq-java-client
cd rabbitmq-java-client
ant dist
```

You can then either include the `rabbitmq-java-VERSION JAR` in the build path of your project (and use it with a testing library such as JUnit or TestNG to build your performance test suite or build a custom tool on top of it) or execute the PerfTest utility directly from the command line and observe statistics. The following example shows the available options for the PerfTest utility in Windows (in a Linux distribution, you can use the `runjava.sh` script alternatively):

```
cd build/dist
runjava.sh com.rabbitmq.examples.PerfTest -help
```

As you can see, it takes into account many of the factors that can affect the performance and we already covered this in this section. In addition, it allows you to set different criteria to conduct performance measurements including the prefilling of queues with messages. It lacks features for the testing of the performance in a cluster, such as setting up mirroring policies or precreating multiple queues with proper distribution over the cluster nodes. However, you can easily build your own tool on top of PerfTest that does that for you. Let's assume that we have our three-node RabbitMQ local cluster up and running. The tool performs the following functions:

- It starts up a number of consumers in separate consumer threads; only one consumer is started by default

- It starts up a number of producers in separate producer threads; only one producer is started by default

- It starts sending messages from the producers and consuming them from the consumers

- It displays the collected statistics for the time period (starting with one second) and the number of sent and consumed messages for this period along with the minimum, average, and maximum latency for a message

Before running the tool, you must take into account several important facts:

- If you specify the number of messages to the publisher, be sure to specify the same or smaller number of messages to be consumed from the consumers; otherwise, the tool will hang and will not display any statistics (at least one consumer will still be waiting for messages). For example, if you have one producer and you want to send 10,000 messages to two consumers, you must specify a value of 50,000 or less for the consumer message count.

- If you specify the number of messages to the producer, be sure to specify a large enough amount of messages (that will require more than a second of processing) in order to get accurate statistics; for a small amount of messages, PerfTest will not give you accurate statistics.

The following example runs the tool with auto-acknowledgment by sending messages from a single producer and binding a single consumer:

```
cd build/dist
runjava.bat com.rabbitmq.examples.PerfTest -a
```

We can observe the following result:

```
starting consumer #0
starting producer #0
time: 1.000s, sent: 23959 msg/s, received: 20884 msg/s, min/avg/max
latency: 210
/65998/93740 microseconds
time: 2.000s, sent: 51274 msg/s, received: 51371 msg/s, min/avg/max
latency: 495
19/59427/94140 microseconds
time: 3.000s, sent: 53224 msg/s, received: 52846 msg/s, min/avg/max
latency: 487
12/57278/68175 microseconds
time: 4.000s, sent: 53228 msg/s, received: 53752 msg/s, min/avg/max
latency: 477
22/56663/65392 microseconds
time: 5.000s, sent: 53878 msg/s, received: 53533 msg/s, min/avg/max
latency: 487
26/57483/70630 microseconds
...
```

You can see that after the first second, we produce and consume roughly about 52,000 messages per second with auto-acknowledgement enabled. Now, let's execute the same test with the acknowledgment of each message from the consumer:

```
runjava.bat com.rabbitmq.examples.PerfTest
```

We can observe the following result:

```
starting consumer #0
starting producer #0
time: 1.000s, sent: 15088 msg/s, received: 11151 msg/s, min/avg/max
latency: 262
6/133696/214058 microseconds
time: 2.001s, sent: 25932 msg/s, received: 23126 msg/s, min/avg/max
latency: 137
341/213911/272298 microseconds
time: 3.001s, sent: 26605 msg/s, received: 22065 msg/s, min/avg/max
latency: 249
500/333672/455356 microseconds
time: 4.002s, sent: 22690 msg/s, received: 19948 msg/s, min/avg/max
latency: 444
164/570170/643165 microseconds
time: 5.002s, sent: 24013 msg/s, received: 20410 msg/s, min/avg/max
latency: 562
357/654099/717019 microseconds
...
```

You can see now that the performance drops more than twice (roughly about 21,000 messages per second) with acknowledgments from the consumer, which is a significant performance hit. Let's also make messages persistent before running the performance measurement:

```
runjava.bat com.rabbitmq.examples.PerfTest -f persistent
```

We can observe the following result:

```
starting consumer #0
starting producer #0
time: 1.004s, sent: 11297 msg/s, received: 6623 msg/s, min/avg/max
latency: 3168
/227397/373579 microseconds
time: 2.006s, sent: 15388 msg/s, received: 11577 msg/s, min/avg/max
latency: 338
389/456810/586714 microseconds
time: 3.006s, sent: 13493 msg/s, received: 10476 msg/s, min/avg/max
latency: 570
519/711663/886369 microseconds
time: 4.006s, sent: 12850 msg/s, received: 9844 msg/s, min/avg/max
latency: 8203
60/1052631/1172428 microseconds
time: 5.010s, sent: 14719 msg/s, received: 11384 msg/s, min/avg/max
latency: 113
1484/1183177/1235015 microseconds
```

This is even worse: about 10,000 messages per second when message persistence takes place. You can specify further options such as publisher confirms, number of consumers/producers, messages, and others depending on your setup and messaging requirements.

The following example allows you to predict what would be the relative time to produce and consume 1,000,000 messages of size 4 KB using a single producer and consumer without acknowledgments:

```
runjava.bat com.rabbitmq.examples.PerfTest -a -C 1000000 -D 1000000 -s
4096
```

On the sample three-node RabbitMQ cluster, it took about 20 seconds to process all the messages.

Monitoring of RabbitMQ instances

We have been discussing various performance tuning tips that would allow us to create a more scalable broker setup. However, in order to be able to observe how our setup behaves in various scenarios, it is not sufficient to do only partial performance measurements using PerfTest, a custom performance tool, or even a third-party performance-testing solution. In a production environment, we would typically want to have a real-time monitoring solution that would allow us to observe how our broker behaves at any point in time enabling us to take measures as fast as possible when something goes wrong with our RabbitMQ instances.

The RabbitMQ management plugin provides you with a good real-time overview of the resource utilization of the instances of a cluster and the message rates per queue or exchange. However, we may want to have a central monitoring infrastructure that monitors all the parts of our infrastructure, including the message broker. Moreover, we may want to make use of advanced features provided by a typical monitoring solution such as the ability to receive notifications (e-mail, SMS, and so on) when something wrong happens with the broker such as a failed RabbitMQ instance or an exceeded memory / CPU / free disk threshold. For this reason, we can leverage a monitoring solution to do the job.

We will briefly discuss the capabilities provided by the management plugin, and then we will see how to monitor RabbitMQ using Nagios, Monit, or Munin assuming that we are running our RabbitMQ instances in a Linux environment.

The management UI

When you navigate to the **Overview** tab of the RabbitMQ management web interface and click on a node, you can observe the resource consumption by this node in real time under the **Statistics** section:

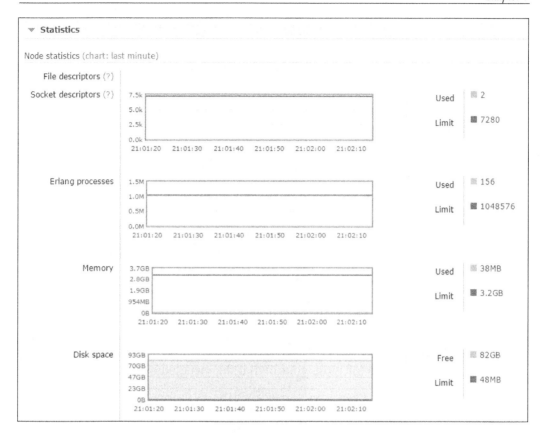

You can observe the number of file descriptors or socket descriptors that are used, Erlang processes, and memory currently used by the message broker along with the current free disk space. On the same page, you can observe more information about the distribution of memory among the different components of the message broker under the **Memory details** section by clicking on the **Update** button first in order to take a memory snapshot:

You can also check the message rates from **Queues** and **Exchanges** by clicking on a particular queue or exchange.

Nagios

Nagios is an open source system monitoring application that provides a number of plugins to extend its capabilities along with various types of integrations with different network protocols and applications. In order to install Nagios in Ubuntu, you can use the following command:

```
sudo apt-get update
sudo apt-get install nagios3 nagios-nrpe-plugin
```

When prompted during the installation, specify a proper password for the Nagios administrative panel. To check whether the Nagios service is running, execute the following command:

```
sudo service nagios3 status
```

You should now be able to log in to the Nagios administrative interface from `http://localhost/nagios3` and provide the `nagiosadmin` user along with the password that you specified during the installation. The next thing to do is to install some Nagios health checks (or write your own if the installed ones are not proper):

```
git clone https://github.com/jamesc/nagios-plugins-rabbitmq
sudo chown -R nagios:nagios nagios-plugins-rabbitmq/
mv nagios-plugins-rabbitmq /usr/lib/nagios/plugins/
sudo apt-get install libnagios-plugin-perl
sudo apt-get install libnagios-object-perl
apt-get install perl-Nagios-Plugin
apt-get install libreadonly-xs-perl
sudp perl -MCPAN -e 'install Bundle::LWP'
perl -MCPAN -e 'install Monitoring::Plugin'
sudo cp -R /usr/share/perl/5.14.2/CPAN/LWP/ /etc/perl/
sudo cpan install JSON
```

In short, the process described in the preceding commands is as follows:

1. We download the sources of the health checks from the **nagios-plugins-rabbitmq** GitHub repository. You can see the available checks (provided as Perl scripts) under the `nagios-plugins-rabbitmq/scripts` directory; they use the RabbitMQ management REST API.

2. We change the permissions of the sources and move them to the Nagios plugins directory.

3. We install the Monitoring:Plugin Perl plugin along with the additional dependencies that is needed in order to write plugins for Nagios under Perl; this is required as the RabbitMQ health checks that we downloaded are provided as Perl scripts that depend on this library.

To verify that you can run a check, you can execute the following:

```
cd nagios-plugins-rabbitmq/scripts
./check_rabbitmq_server
```

If you are prompted to provide a hostname, then check whether your compiles are fine. You need to define a particular command using this script in the `commands.cfg` configuration file of Nagios:

```
sudo vim /etc/nagios3/commands.cfg
define command {
 command_name check_rabbitmq_server
 command_line /usr/lib/nagios/plugins/nagios-plugins-rabbitmq/scripts/
check_rabbitmq_server -H localhost --port=15672 -u guest -p guest
 }
```

You can now restart the service with the following:

```
sudo service nagios3 restart
```

When you navigate to the **Configuration** menu under the **System** section, select **Commands** from the dropdown and click on **view**; you should see the `you check-rabbitmq-server` command in the list. In a similar way, you can define the other already provided RabbitMQ checks if you need them to monitor.

You can create a service definition that uses the command and allows you to specify which groups you would like to notify, for example, in case the RabbitMQ server goes down. You can do this with the other RabbitMQ health checks as well. You can also write your own health checks for RabbitMQ, for example, using Java and RabbitMQ management REST API or the `rabbitmqctl` utility.

Monit

Monit is a Unix utility to monitor processes. You can also use it to monitor the RabbitMQ instance process in a pretty straightforward manner. Monit requires a `pid` file that stores the process ID for the currently running process. In the earlier versions of the rabbitmq-server script `init script under /etc/init.d`, you had to add the creation and deletion of this `pid` file manually upon the service startup/shutdown. However, the later versions of RabbitMQ store a `pid` file for the RabbitMQ Erlang process under the `/var/run/rabbitmq/pid` directory.

In order to install Monit, execute the following command:

```
sudo apt-get install monit
```

You can then add the following configuration to the `/etc/monit/monitrc` file in order to monitor the RabbitMQ process from the localhost:

```
set httpd port 2812 and
use address localhost
allow localhost
allow @monit
allow @users readonly

CHECK PROCESS rabbitmq-server WITH PIDFILE /var/run/rabbitmq/pid
  GROUP rabbitmq
  START PROGRAM "/usr/sbin/service rabbitmq-server start"
  STOP PROGRAM "/usr/sbin/service rabbitmq-server stop"
  IF DOES NOT EXIST FOR 3 CYCLES THEN RESTART
  IF FAILED PORT 5672 4 TIMES WITHIN 6 CYCLES THEN RESTART
```

You can start monit in the background with the following command:

sudo service monit start

sudo monit

You can then check the status of the monited processes (including the Erlang process of RabbitMQ) using the following command:

sudo monit status

You should see an output similar to the following:

```
Process 'rabbitmq-server'
  status                        Running
  monitoring status             Monitored
  pid                           1046
  parent pid                    1039
```

```
uptime                          6d 12h 6m
children                        2
memory kilobytes                13680
memory kilobytes total          14484
memory percent                  0.6%
memory percent total            0.7%
cpu percent                     0.0%
cpu percent total               0.0%
port response time              0.000s to localhost:5672 [DEFAULT
via TCP]
data collected                  Mon, 31 Aug 2015 01:47:59
```

Munin

You can use Munin as a nice alternative to Nagios for the monitoring. The following command installs Munin in Ubuntu (note that the Apache HTTP server must also be installed):

```
sudo apt-get install apache2
sudo apt-get install munin
```

You must then edit the Munin configuration:

```
vim /etc/munin/munin.conf
```

Uncomment the following and change the value of the htmldir attribute to /var/www/munin:

```
dbdir   /var/lib/munin
htmldir /var /www/munin
logdir /var/log/munin
rundir  /var/run/munin

tmpldir /etc/munin/templates
```

Add the following to the Munin configuration file in order to enable monitoring on the localhost:

```
[MuninMonitor]
    address 127.0.0.1
    use_node_name yes
```

Open the Munin Apache configuration and change the alias to allow external connections:

```
sudo vim /etc/munin/apache.conf
Alias /munin /var/www/munin
<Directory /var/www/munin>
    Order allow,deny
    #Allow from localhost 127.0.0.0/8  ::1
    Allow from all
    Options None
```

Create the `/var/www/munin` directory, change permissions to the munin user and group, and finally restart the apache2 and `munin-node` services:

```
sudo mkdir /var/www/munin
sudo chown munin:munin /var/www/munin
sudo service munin-node restart
sudo service apache2 restart
```

If you navigate to `http://localhost/munin/`, you should be able to see the Munin administrative interface:

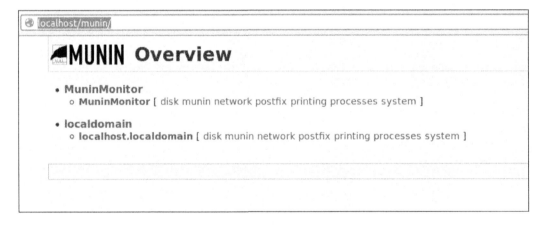

Now, we need to install the Munin RabbitMQ set of plugins. To do so, execute the following commands in order to download the Munin plugins directly to the Munin plugins directory:

```
cd /etc/munin/plugins/
sudo git clone https://github.com/ask/rabbitmq-munin
sudo cp rabbitmq-munin/* .
```

Add the following configuration to the `/etc/munin/plugin-conf.d/munin-node` file:

```
sudo vim /etc/munin/plugin-conf.d/munin-node
[rabbitmq_connections]
user root

[rabbitmq_consumers]
user root

[rabbitmq_messages]
user root

[rabbitmq_messages_unacknowledged]
user root

[rabbitmq_messages_uncommitted]
user root

[rabbitmq_queue_memory]
user root
```

Finally, restart the `munin-node` service and check whether you have the munin plugins available from the administrative interface:

```
sudo service munin-node restart
```

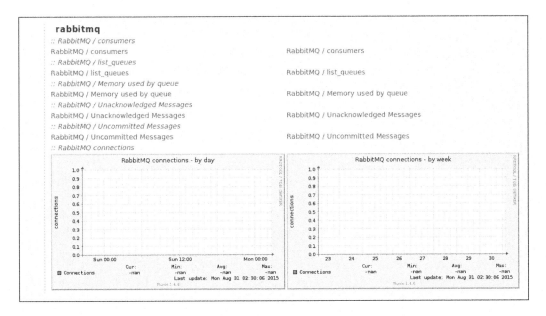

Comparing RabbitMQ with other message brokers

It is not uncommon that when it comes to choosing a message broker for your system, you may not choose RabbitMQ as a proper solution without any comparison with other message brokers. Although RabbitMQ is a great technology, it can turn out that there is a better message broker (either in turns of features or performance) based on your requirements. For this reason, you can benchmark RabbitMQ against other message brokers such as Qpid, ActiveMQ, ZeroMQ, HornetMQ, and Kafka, just to name a few. For this, you can follow the approach provided by the PerfTest tool and build a wrapper utility (that can abstract PerfTest for RabbitMQ) that allows you to produce and consume messages of different numbers and sizes on each of the brokers that you would like to benchmark along with RabbitMQ.

Case Study : Performance tuning and monitoring of RabbitMQ instances in CSN

The CSN team decided to scale the system both vertically and horizontally in terms of the RabbitMQ message broker by introducing more RAM and disk space on each of the RabbitMQ instance servers and change the RabbitMQ configuration parameters accordingly so that the broker can use more memory and disk space, if needed. The team also decided to introduce more RAM nodes for the chat queues along with a deployment of Nagios to monitor all the parts of the system (including the message broker) and send notifications to the team in case of issues with resource utilization based on defined thresholds.

Summary

In this chapter, we provided a list of performance tuning tips that can be used to build a proper approach for the tuning of the performance of the RabbitMQ message broker. We discussed how to measure the performance using the **PerfTest** utility provided by the RabbitMQ Java client and monitor the performance in real time using either the management interface or third-party monitoring solution, such as Nagios, Monit, or Munin. At the end, we discussed how we can compare the performance of RabbitMQ against a few other message brokers that are widely used in practice and compete against RabbitMQ.

Exercises

1. How can you optimize the performance of a single RabbitMQ instance?

2. How can you optimize the performance of a single RabbitMQ cluster?

3. How do acknowledgments and publisher confirms affect the performance?

4. What tool can you use to measure the performance of a RabbitMQ instance?

5. How can you set memory and disk free limits per RabbitMQ instance?

6. What is QoS prefetching and how does it affect the performance?

7. How do message persistence and message TTL affect the performance?

8. How can you monitor memory, disk, and CPU consumption of a RabbitMQ instance?

9. How can you evaluate RabbitMQ against other message brokers in terms of performance?

10. Is RabbitMQ better than ActiveMQ or ZeroMQ in terms of performance?

8
Troubleshooting

Running and maintaining a system successfully requires a good understanding of its components along with the various utilities that can be used to troubleshoot problems occurring in any of these components. In this chapter, we will look into some techniques that can be applied to troubleshoot the problem that is occurring with your RabbitMQ instances along with several common issues occurring in practice.

The topics to be covered in the chapter are as follows:

- General troubleshooting approach
- Problems with starting/stopping the RabbitMQ nodes
- Problems with message delivery

General troubleshooting approach

As RabbitMQ instances run on top of the Erlang virtual machine, we can leverage the troubleshooting utilities provided by Erlang to troubleshoot problems occurring in the message broker. The variety of errors occurring may range from problems relating to starting/stopping the broker instance to performance issues—we already covered performance tuning and monitoring in the previous chapter; therefore, you can already apply that knowledge to troubleshooting. We will use a **top-down** approach to troubleshoot issues, as follows:

1. Check the status of a particular node.
2. Inspect RabbitMQ logs.
3. Check the RabbitMQ community mailing list or ask in the IRC chat.
4. Use Erlang utilities to troubleshoot a particular node.

Checking the status of a particular node

You can check the status of a particular node using the `rabbitmq` utility as follows:

```
rabbitmqctl.bat -n instance1 status
```

In the preceding example, we are checking the status of the `instance1` RabbitMQ node. You will observe an output of the `status` command similar to the following (we are omitting resource-related statistics, such as memory usage and number of processes, as we already covered them in the previous chapter):

```
[{pid,10312},
 {running_applications,
     [{rabbitmq_shovel,"Data Shovel for RabbitMQ","3.4.4"},
      {rabbitmq_management_agent,"RabbitMQ Management Agent","3.4.4"},
      {rabbit,"RabbitMQ","3.4.4"},
      {os_mon,"CPO  CXC 138 46","2.3"},
      {gen_smtp,"An erlang SMTP server/client framework",
          "0.9.0-rmq3.4.x-61e19ec5-gita62c02e"},
      {ssl,"Erlang/OTP SSL application","5.3.8"},
      {public_key,"Public key infrastructure","0.22.1"},
      {crypto,"CRYPTO","3.4.2"},
      {mnesia,"MNESIA  CXC 138 12","4.12.4"},
      {amqp_client,"RabbitMQ AMQP Client","3.4.4"},
      {xmerl,"XML parser","1.3.7"},
      {asn1,"The Erlang ASN1 compiler version 3.0.3","3.0.3"},
      {sasl,"SASL  CXC 138 11","2.4.1"},
      {stdlib,"ERTS  CXC 138 10","2.3"},
      {kernel,"ERTS  CXC 138 10","3.1"}]},
 {os,{win32,nt}},
 {erlang_version,
     "Erlang/OTP 17 [erts-6.3] [64-bit] [smp:8:8] [async-
threads:30]\n"}
```

In the preceding piece of output, you can observe a lot of useful information, such as the following:

- RabbitMQ message broker version
- Erlang distribution
- Operating system
- RabbitMQ Erlang applications along with their versions

This is a good starting point to troubleshoot.

Inspecting the RabbitMQ logs

The RabbitMQ logs are located in the `logs` directory by default in the RabbitMQ installation directory in Windows or in the `/var/log/rabbitmq` directory in Unix-like operating systems. This location can be changed by setting the `RABBITMQ_LOG_BASE` environment variable. You can inspect the error logs for more detailed errors that are related to either the particular instance or in regard to communication with other nodes in the cluster. The RabbitMQ logs can be rotated using the `rabbitmqctl` utility with the `rotate_logs` command. Along with the RabbitMQ log file for the node, there is an alternative log file (ending with an **SASL** suffix), which is generated by the Erlang **SASL (System Architecture Support Libraries)** application libraries that provide different forms of logging reports, including crash reports.

The following message specifies that free disk monitoring (required for comparison against the free disk threshold, set by the `disk_free_limit` configuration parameter) is not supported on the platform that runs the RabbitMQ node:

```
=INFO REPORT==== 2-Sep-2015::20:41:47 ===
Disabling disk free space monitoring on unsupported platform:
{{'EXIT',{eacces,[{erlang,open_port,
                        [{spawn,"C:\\Windows\\system32\\cmd.exe /c
dir /-C /W \"d:/software/RabbitMQ/rabbitmq_server-3.4.4/db/rabbit@
DOMAIN-mnesia\""},
                        [stream,in,eof,hide]],
                        []},
                  {os,cmd,1,[{file,"os.erl"},{line,204}]},
                  {rabbit_disk_monitor,get_disk_free,2,[]},
                  {rabbit_disk_monitor,init,1,[]},
                  {gen_server,init_it,6,[{file,"gen_server.
erl"},{line,306}]},
                  {proc_lib,init_p_do_apply,3,
                        [{file,"proc_lib.erl"},{line,237}]}]}}},
```

In this particular example, the message is descriptive enough and can save you the effort of looking further in the Erlang stack trace. In the SASL log file, the same error looks similar to the following:

```
=CRASH REPORT==== 2-Sep-2015::20:41:45 ===
  crasher:
    initial call: rabbit_disk_monitor:init/1
    pid: <0.28939.1>
    registered_name: []
    exception exit: unsupported_platform
      in function  gen_server:init_it/6 (gen_server.erl, line 322)
    ancestors: [rabbit_disk_monitor_sup,rabbit_sup,<0.143.0>]
    messages: []
```

```
    links: [<0.262.0>]
    dictionary: []
    trap_exit: false
    status: running
    heap_size: 1598
    stack_size: 27
    reductions: 646
  neighbours:
```

If you are trying to consume a message from a non-existent queue (for example, **test-queue**), you may see a message such as the following in the logs:

```
=ERROR REPORT==== 20-Jul-2015::12:31:20 ===
Channel error on connection <0.514.0> (127.0.0.1:63451 ->
127.0.0.1:5672, vhost: '/', user: 'guest'), channel 2:
{amqp_error,not_found,"no queue 'test-queue' in vhost '/'",'basic.
consume'}
```

In case you lose a connection with a cluster node, you will get a message that can be easily interpreted, as follows:

```
=ERROR REPORT==== 2-Sep-2015::23:12:27 ===
** Node instance1@Domain not responding **
** Removing (timedout) connection **
```

In case you are running a RabbitMQ cluster and you already have the web management console started on the default port, you can hit the following problem (as displayed in the RabbitMQ log file):

```
=ERROR REPORT==== 20-Jul-2015::12:25:41 ===
** Generic server rabbit_web_dispatch_registry terminating
** Last message in was {add,rabbit_mgmt,
                        [{port,15672}],
                        #Fun<rabbit_web_dispatch.1.31447083>,
                        #Fun<rabbit_mgmt_app.0.15521781>,
                        {[],"RabbitMQ Management"}}
** When Server state == undefined
** Reason for termination ==
** {{could_not_start_listener,[{port,15672}],eaddrinuse},
    [{rabbit_web_dispatch_sup,check_error,2,[]},
     {rabbit_web_dispatch_registry,handle_call,3,[]},
     {gen_server,try_handle_call,4,[{file,"gen_server.
erl"},{line,607}]},
     {gen_server,handle_msg,5,[{file,"gen_server.erl"},{line,639}]},
     {proc_lib,init_p_do_apply,3,[{file,"proc_lib.erl"},{line,237}]}]}
```

This indicates that `15672` could not be opened (if another cluster node is running the management console, you do not need to enable it for other cluster nodes anyway, unless you want to specify a different port on which you want to run the management plugin for the purpose of high availability). However, if the `15672` port is not in use, this may indicate a mismatch between the Erlang distribution and the RabbitMQ server, preventing the management plugin to open the `15672` port. This leads us to use alternative mechanisms for further troubleshooting of the problem.

The RabbitMQ mailing list and IRC channel

At this point, you may have already discovered the output of the `status` command and inspected the logs; however, you might still be clueless about what the reason for the error that we saw in the previous section could be:

```
** Generic server rabbit_web_dispatch_registry terminating
```

Now, you may look for a similar issue on the **rabbitmq-users** or **rabbitmq-discuss** mailing lists. If you don't find a similar issue suggested with a proper solution for the problem, you can drop a message to the mailing list describing your problem in detail and sending the RabbitMQ logs, along with the Erlang crash dump. The Erlang crash dump file is generated when the Erlang VM abnormally terminates, and it is generated in the directory where your RabbitMQ server starts (for example, the `sbin` directory from the RabbitMQ installation in Windows).

Erlang troubleshooting

The `erl_crash.dump` file is created in the startup directory of the RabbitMQ server when something goes wrong with the message broker. It is not the only means by which you can troubleshoot the message broker using information that is provided by the Erlang runtime, you can also directly connect to the Erlang process of the RabbitMQ instance and query it for the purpose of troubleshooting.

An Erlang Primer

To be able to dig into the root cause of a problem requires a good understanding of the Erlang programming language. In this section, we will cover the basics of Erlang and make use of this knowledge in the last chapter of the book, when we discuss how to create a plugin for RabbitMQ and how to implement RabbitMQ.

To begin, you need to add the `<erlang_home>\bin` directory to your `PATH` and execute the following command from the command line:

```
erl
```

The command will fire up the Erlang **REPL** (**Read-Eval-Print-Loop**) shell, where you can type the Erlang commands. To connect to a particular node that is running on the local workstation, you can provide the domain name of the instance with the `-sname` option (sname stands for 'short names' and it is the default instance-naming format that RabbitMQ uses), as shown in the following:

```
erl -sname rabbit@DOMAIN
```

In order to use the preceding command, you need to stop the `rabbit@DOMAIN` node first.

You can start by evaluating the following expression using the Erlang interpreter (don't forget the dot at the end of each expression):

```
(4 + 6) * 2.
```

Not only can the arithmetic expressions be evaluated. Let's transform the preceding example using two variables, as follows:

```
X = 4.
Y = 6.
(X + Y) * 2.
```

If you reassign the X variable to 10, as follows:

```
X = 10.
```

You will get an error as shown in the following:

```
** exception error: no match of right hand side value 10
```

To reassign the variable, you need to first unbind it using the `f()` function:

```
f(X).
```

Note that you can unbind all variables by simply calling the following function:

```
f().
```

The preceding expression is not of much use; therefore, let's make a function out of it from the Erlang shell:

```
F = fun(X,Y) -> (X + Y) * 2 end.
```

The `fun` keyword can be used to define an anonymous function. In the previous case, this function is bound to the F variable. Now, you can evaluate the former expression using the following function:

```
F(4,6).
```

Functions in Erlang are typically defined in modules. A module in Erlang is defined as a file with an .erl extension, which is further compiled to an Erlang object file with a **.beam** extension that represents the actual byte code that is executed by the Erlang virtual machine. You can define the preceding function in a module called **sample** (saved in a sample.erl file. Please note that the name of the file should match the module declaration):

```
-module(sample).
-export([double/2]).
double(X,Y) -> (X+Y) * 2.
```

The –module declaration specifies the name of the module, followed by one or more -export declarations that explicitly specify which functions from the module are exported by the module and can be used by other modules. You should specify the name of the function along with its arity (number of parameters that the function accepts). Functions with the same name but different numbers of parameters are treated as separate function declarations by Erlang. In the module, there is a double function—this declaration is valid only in a module and cannot be executed from the shell—you should use the **fun** keyword for this, as we saw earlier.

To compile the module, you must first navigate to the directory of your module using the cd() function and then, the c() function, to compile the module to a beam file. Assuming the sample.erl file is created in the D:\sources directory, you can execute the following from the Erlang REPL in order to compile the module:

```
cd('D:/sources').(sample).
```

If compilation is successful, you will see a message as follows:

```
{ok,sample}
```

This is actually a tuple that is returned from the c() function, which indicates a successful status (ok) and the name of the compiled module. A tuple, in Erlang, is a container with a fixed number of elements that can be of different types. In order to invoke the double function from the sample module, you can write the following:

```
sample:double(6,4).
```

Use the m() function or the module_info() method (which returns a list with the result) that is available for each Erlang module to check for information, such as available functions, about the module:

```
m(sample).
sample:module_info().
```

These can also be pretty useful utilities to inspect the existing modules in a system such as RabbitMQ.

Variable definitions do not specify the type of the variable, it is determined at runtime (as seen in the `double` function). We have the following types of data:

- `integers`: There is no limit to the size of an integer in Erlang, for example, 257.
- `floats`: For example, 45.6.
- `atoms`: They are used to create constants; you can think of them as values of an enumeration or constant, for example, X, Y.
- `booleans`: **true** or **false**.
- `references`: They are used to create unique identifiers for objects.
- `bit strings`: They are used to represent sequences of bits as segments of particular value that optionally have a length and a type, for example, << <<0:1,1:1, 0:1>>. In this particular example, the bit string represents the bit sequence "010". Bit strings are very useful to parse binary streams of data, for example, parsing a protocol message based on a protocol mask. As you can see, this mechanism can be directly used to parse an AMQP message.
- `binaries`: They are simply bit strings, where each segment of the string is a sequence of bits that is divisible by eight. For example, <<111, 172, 15>>.
- `pids`: They are used to represent process identifiers.
- `ports`: They are used to represent Erlang ports; essentially a separate processes is started for an Erlang process that maps to an OS port and provides a communication with the external world.
- `funs`: They are used to create function objects (closures).
- `tuples`: They are containers for a fixed number of items, possibly of different types.
- `lists`: They are containers for a variable number of items, possibly of different types.
- `maps`: They are containers for a key-value pair of items.
- `records`: They are containers for a mixed type of data, similar to C structs and compiled to tuples.

Erlang uses the concept of pattern matching in order to bind one or more variables to the particular values. It is used to assign variables (denoted by atoms) using more complex expressions that direct assignment. Consider the following examples:

```
{X,b} = {a,b}.
[10,[Y],15] = [10,[[1,2,3]],15].
{X,X} = {a,b}.
[A,2] = [10].
```

The first expression binds X to a, the second expressions binds Y to the [1,2,3] list, and the third and fourth expressions result in exceptions as pattern matching fails in these cases. We will briefly cover error handling later in the chapter.

Another useful concept is list comprehensions, where you can iterate over a list and return a modified list using a filter function and a generator for the elements of the new list. Consider the following example:

```
[X+1 || X <- [4,5,6], X rem 2 == 0].
```

The result is the [5,7] list, all even elements are filtered and incremented by one in the new list. We can rewrite the preceding example using a recursive function, as Erlang enforces the functional programming style along with idioms derived from languages such as Prolog; the language does not provide a looping construct. The filter_list_sample function implements the same behavior as the list comprehension using an if statement:

```
filter_list_sample(L) -> filter_list_sample_helper(L, []).
filter_list_sample_helper([], Res) -> Res.
filter_list_sample_helper([X|L], Res) ->
if
    X rem 2 == 0 ->
    filter_list_sample_helper(L, [X+1| Res]).
    true ->
        filter_list_sample_helper(L, Res)
end.
```

If you add this to the sample module that we created earlier, export the filter_list_sample function from the module, and recompile it, you can invoke the preceding function with the following:

```
sample:filter_list_sample([4,5,6]).
```

The result is returned in reverse order due to the recursion; implement a function that reverses the resulting list as an exercise. Note that if you have multiple definitions of the same function (in this case, filter_list_sample_helper), you should separate them with a semicolon. Multiple expressions in the same function are separated by a comma. You can also use the case expression instead of the if expression in the preceding example, as shown in the following:

```
filter_list_sample_helper([X|L], Res) ->
case X rem 2 of
0 -> filter_list_sample_helper(L, [X+1| Res]).
    _ -> filter_list_sample_helper(L, Res)
end.
```

The underscore (_) indicates any match (in this case, this could be only 1).

There are many scenarios where Erlang may throw an error, and we can differentiate between the three types of runtime errors, as follows:

1. **regular errors**: Thrown by an `erlang:error()` call. This is the equivalent of a `throw` statement in the programming languages such as C++ or Java, stacktrace is included as a part of the error.

2. **throw errors**: Thrown by a `throw()` function. This is typically used to exit a deeply nested function call and does include a stacktrace rather it includes a value that was handled earlier in the call stack.

3. **exit errors**: Thrown by an `erlang:exit()` call. This is used to signal that a process is exiting (a value of `normal` passed to the function indicates that the process exits normally, other exit codes indicate an error).

All the types of errors can be caught using a `try ... catch` block. The following example demonstrates the use of the different types of exceptions in Erlang:

```erlang
exception_sample(Val) ->
    case Val of
        1 -> throw("Invalid value: 1").
        2 -> error("Invalid value: 2").
        3 -> exit("Invalid value: 3").
        _ -> "Success"
    end.

exception_handler(Val) ->
    try
        exception_sample(Val)
    catch
        error: Error -> {error, Error}.
        throw: Error -> {throw, Error}.
        exit: Error -> {exit, Error}
    end.
```

Export the `exception_handler()` function as part of the sample module and execute it with different arguments to see how it behaves:

```erlang
sample:exception_handler(1).
sample:exception_handler(2).
sample:exception_handler(3).
sample:exception_handler(4).
```

You should receive the following output:

```
{throw,"Invalid value: 1"}
{error,"Invalid value: 2"}
{exit,"Invalid value: 3"}
"Success"
```

When an Erlang process exits as a result of an error that is not handled by the process, you will get a result that is in a format similar to the RabbitMQ node crashing as RabbitMQ nodes are started as Erlang processes.

So far, we discussed the basic constructs of the language. However, Erlang excels when it comes to distributed programming. Processes in Erlang are lightweight, they are created by the Erlang VM without actually interacting with the underlying operating system (and creating any OS-level threads or processes). Communication between processes is possible via message passing. The Erlang VM takes the responsibility of handling the process execution underneath on one or more CPUs in the system on which the Erlang VM runs. Thus, reducing context switching' you don't need to go to the kernel scheduler to switch between the currently executing threads. This, and the ability to dynamically allocate process stacks (thus saving the effort to reserve a lot of RAM), provides the possibility of creating thousands of Erlang processes at once. If any two processes need to communicate on the same machine, you can do it directly using the ! and `receive` expression in order to exchange messages, as demonstrated in the following example:

```
sample_sender(Pid, Message) ->
    Pid ! Message.

sample_receiver() ->
    receive
        Message -> io:format(Message, [])
    end.

start() ->
    Preceiver = spawn(?MODULE, sample_receiver, []),
    spawn(?MODULE, sample_sender, [Preceiver, "Test message."]).
```

We create a sender and receiver as separate processes in the `start()` method using the `spawn` function that creates a process based on a module function, along with the parameter passed to that function upon process creation. The `?MODULE` macros refer to the current module, you can think of the Erlang macros as C++ preprocessor directives. The `sample_sender()` function sends a message using the `!` operator to the process identified by a particular **pid (proportional–integral–derivative)**. The `sample_receiver()` method uses the `receive` expression to wait for a message and is blocked until a message is received. The message is printed on the standard output using the built-in `io:format` Erlang function. You need to export all the three functions from the `sample` module and run the demo using the following line of code from the Erlang REPL:

```
sample:start().
```

In this particular example, the processes run in the same Erlang VM. However, if the processes are started on a remote machine, then several concerns are further raised. The most important issues to solve are as follows:

- How do we exchange the process identifiers among the processes? How are the processes aware of each other?

- How can you prevent tampering of communication from a third party among the processes?

The answer to the first question is the `register()` built-in function that allows you to map a symbolic name to a process identifier. This mapping information is stored in an Erlang register, and when a process needs to communicate with another remote process, it must know the address of the machine where the other process resides along with the symbolic name of the remote process. The rest is handled by Erlang behind the scenes.

The answer to the second question is the Erlang cookies that we mentioned in the earlier chapters when we talked about RabbitMQ clustering. Erlang cookies are stored in an `.erlang.cookie` file and are used by the Erlang processes as a shared secret. A node is not obliged to use the same cookie for all other remote nodes—a different cookie can be specified for communication with a remote node. This can be accomplished using the `erlang:set_cookie()` method that uses the remote node identifier and Erlang cookie instance as arguments. To retrieve the current cookie used by the node, you can use the `erlang:get_cookie()` method. In case no cookie is in use, the method will return `nocookie`.

Our brief primer of the Erlang language should be sufficient in order to make use of the utilities provided by the language for further troubleshooting of your RabbitMQ instances. You can retrieve the name of the current node with the following command:

```
node().
```

You can also retrieve the names and the ports of the processes that are registered by the **EPMD (Erlang Port Mapper Daemon)** process running on the same Erlang VM:

```
net_adm:names().
```

Assuming that we have started our three-node cluster on the same machine, we should observe the following output:

```
{ok,[{"rabbit",25672},
     {"instance1",25701},
     {"instance2",25702}]}
```

The ports that you see for each node are the ports assigned to the Erlang processes for each RabbitMQ instance (in the previous case, 20000 + the name of the RabbiqMQ instance port).

We can also use the `rpc:call` function in order to execute a function in a particular local/remote Erlang process (and this could be the process of a RabbitMQ instance). You can also use the different Erlang utilities, such as the `rpc:call()` function, to execute the commands on remote processes or retrieve the information about these processes.

The Erlang crash dump

The Erlang crash dump file is created in the current working directory of a Rabbit instance when it crashes. The crash dump file contains useful statistics that are collected at the time of the crash along with the information about the processes that are affected as part of the crash. The reason for the node failure is indicated by the line starting with the word **slogan**. For example, the following command indicates that there is a problem with starting up of a node (without providing more details as a part of the reason):

```
Slogan: init terminating in do_boot ()
```

You can use the knowledge gained from the previous section to inspect the information that is collected in the crash dump or better, use the **Crashdump Viewer** GUI utility to inspect the crash dump. To start the utility, invoke the following commnad from the Erlang REPL:

```
crashdump_viewer:start().
```

After the tool is started, you will be prompted to select the crash dump file. After the file is selected, the tool will divide the information from the file into proper sections and tables for easier inspection, as follows:

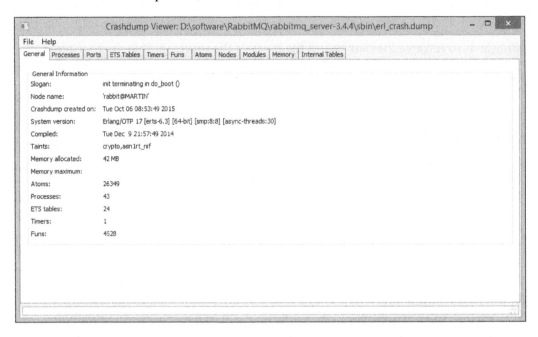

We will expand further on the concept of troubleshooting when we discuss the internal architecture of the message broker. If you get an error that contains: `init terminating in do_boot()`, then there are several things that might be the root cause of the problem (make sure that you analyze the crash dump for more information on the problem):

- Insufficient permissions on some of the RabbitMQ folders and files.
- Corrupt RabbitMQ database. In this case, delete the contents of the `%APPDATA%\RabbitMQ` folder (in Windows) and restore it using a recent backup, if this is at all possible.
- Check the version of your Erlang installation and if it does not match your OS architecture (32/64-bit), reinstall it.

Problems with starting/stopping RabbitMQ nodes

Consider that you have configured a running cluster with three nodes and one of your nodes suddenly fails. When you try to bring up that node using the following:

rabbitmq-server.bat

You get the dreadful BOOT FAILED message along with an error description message of timeout_waiting_for_tables and an Erlang stacktrace, as follows:

```
##########
                Starting broker...

BOOT FAILED
===========

Error description:
    {boot_step,database,
        {error,
            {timeout_waiting_for_tables,
                [rabbit_user,rabbit_user_permission,rabbit_vhost,
                 rabbit_durable_route,rabbit_durable_exchange,
                 rabbit_runtime_parameters,rabbit_durable_queue]}}}

Log files (may contain more information):
    D:/software/RabbitMQ/rabbitmq_server-3.4.4/log/rabbit@MARTIN.log
    D:/software/RabbitMQ/rabbitmq_server-3.4.4/log/rabbit@MARTIN-sasl.
log

Stack trace:
    [{rabbit_table,wait,1,[]},
     {rabbit_table,check_schema_integrity,0,[]},
     {rabbit_mnesia,ensure_schema_integrity,0,[]},
     {rabbit_mnesia,init_db,3,[]},
     {rabbit_mnesia,init_db_and_upgrade,3,[]},
     {rabbit_mnesia,init,0,[]},
     {rabbit,'-run_step/3-lc$^1/1-1-',2,[]},
     {rabbit,run_step,3,[]}]
```

The error message tells you that there is something wrong while loading the data from the Mnesia database; however, it doesn't give you enough information on the exact cause of the problem. One thing you can do is that you can simply remove the node database files from the `rabbit@DOMAIN-mnesia` and `rabbit@DOMAIN-plugins-expand` folders that provide the storage of the Mnesia tables and the expanded plugins that are used by the RabbitMQ node. If you have a recent backup of your Mnesia database, you can try to use it to restore your database data. However, if using a backup is not an option, you need to perform some more troubleshooting in order to find and fix the problem. The first obvious thing to do is to inspect the RabbitMQ logs, as suggested earlier. However, doing so may not always give you more information than the error log that is displayed in the console. Moreover, there is a chance that your Mnesia database is not corrupt. You can try the following options:

- If you are running a single (non-clustered) RabbitMQ node, you may try to specify the full RabbitMQ node name, along with the hostname (if you have changed the hostname of the machine on which you startup your nodes, you may get `timeout_waiting_for_tables` when Mnesia tries to fire up), as follows:

  ```
  set RABBITMQ_NODENAME=rabbit@<DOMAIN>
  ```

- If you are running the node in a clustered environment and the other nodes have not started, the RabbitMQ node may wait for the other nodes to start by default within 30 seconds before throwing a `timeout_waiting_for_tables` error message. In that case, you can try to startup the other nodes in the cluster in 30 seconds from starting the current node and see if this resolves the problem.

Another common issue that may prevent the startup of clustered nodes is network partitioning. Consider that you can have a two- or three-node cluster and the communication links between the nodes fail. Each node becomes isolated from the other and thinks that the other nodes have failed and hence, becomes a master node. If you fix the communication links between the nodes and try to restart them, RabbitMQ will detect that there is more than one master node and startup of nodes may fail with an `incosistent database, running_partitioned_network` error message on subsequent master nodes that try to startup and join the cluster. You can detect this condition by running the following command:

```
rabbitmqctl.bat cluster_status
```

If you see a non–empty partition in the `partitions` attribute from the log, then a network partitioning was detected by RabbitMQ. In normal circumstances, this list is empty:

```
Cluster status of node rabbit@DOMAIN...
[{nodes,[{disc,[instance1@Domain,instance2@Domain,rabbit@DOMAIN]}]},
```

```
{running_nodes, [instance2@Domain, instance1@Martin, rabbit@DOMAIN]},
{cluster_name, <<"rabbit@Domain">>},
{partitions, []}]
```

While each node can act as a standalone master, this means that it may define new exchanges, queues, and bindings without the knowledge of other nodes. However, if you want to restore the cluster, you need to select one node as the master and rejoin the others to the cluster using this node. Before rejoining a node to the cluster, you may also want to reset its state. Assuming that the rabbit@DOMAIN node is your preferred master node, you can issue the following commands to rejoin the instance1 node to the cluster:

```
rabbitmqctl -n instance1 stop_app
rabbitmqctl -n instance1 reset
rabbitmqctl -n instance1 join_cluster rabbit@DOMAIN
rabbitmqctl -n instance1 start_app
```

For more information on network partitioning, you can refer to the **Network Partitions** entry in the RabbitMQ server documentation.

Another reason that your node may fail to startup is due to a resource that is already used by another RabbitMQ instance running on the same machine. If this is a network port that is already taken by the first instance, then the second instance will fail to start. If the first instance is running, for example, the management plugin on a default port and you try to start the second instance with the management plugin enabled, you will get an error message similar to the following:

```
##########
Starting broker...

BOOT FAILED
===========

Error description:
   {could_not_start, rabbitmq_management,
   {could_not_start_listener, [{port, 15672}], eaddrinuse}}

Log files (may contain more information):
   D:/software/RabbitMQ/rabbitmq_server-3.4.4/log/instance1 .log
   D:/software/RabbitMQ/rabbitmq_server-3.4.4/log/instance1 -sasl.log

{"init terminating in do_boot", {rabbit, failure_during_boot, {could_not_
start, rabb
```

```
itmq_management,{could_not_start_listener,[{port,15672}],eaddrinu
se}}}}

Crash dump was written to: erl_crash.dump
init terminating in do_boot ()
```

This is easily solved by disabling the management plugin for that instance. Assuming that this is the instance1 instance, you can execute the following before starting the node:

```
rabbitmq-plugins.bat -n instance1 disable rabbitmq_management
```

As discussed in the earlier chapters, the management plugin is aware of clustering.

Problems with message delivery

In certain broker configurations, it may happen that the messages are not delivered as expected. This could either be due to a misconfigured queue TTL, or a poor network combined with the lack of publisher confirms, or AMQP transactions to support reliable delivery. To inspect what is going on with messages in the broker, you can install the `Firehose` plugin that allows you to inspect the traffic flowing through the message broker. You should be careful when enabling the plugin in a production environment as it may slow down the performance due to the additional messages that it sends to the `amq.rabbitmq.trace` exchange for each message entering the broker and each message exiting it. The plugin is enabled for a particular node and `vhost`. The **RabbitMQ Tracer** plugin builds on top of the Firehose plugin and provides a user interface to capture and trace messages. You can review the additional configuration options for both the plugins in the RabbitMQ documentation.

Summary

In this chapter, we covered the essential mechanisms to troubleshoot the problems that may occur as part of a RabbitMQ instance. We discussed a general approach towards troubleshooting, along with an overview of some common problems that may occur during startup or shutdown of the message broker. For more detailed troublshooting, we introduced the fundamentals of the Erlang programming language and we will reuse that knowledge when we discuss how to extend RabbitMQ. In the next chapter, we will further expand on the concepts that are covered in this chapter by discussing how to troubleshoot security-related issues.

Exercises

1. How does the concept of troubleshooting apply in terms of RabbitMQ?

2. What problems may occur during the startup/shutdown of the message broker?

3. What are the funs in Erlang?

4. How is Erlang handling the process creation?

5. What type of runtime exceptions do we have in Erlang?

6. How is an Erlang module created and compiled?

7. What information does the Erlang crash dump contain?

8. What is the Firehose plugin used for?

9
Security

A system is as secure as its weakest component taking the message broker into account. As RabbitMQ instances can be used to carry sensitive application data or affect the stability of an entire system, we need to make sure that our RabbitMQ deployments are secured properly.

The topics covered in this chapter are as follows:

- Types of threats
- Authentication
- Authorization
- Secure communication
- Penetration testing

Types of threats

There are several aspects in which the security of the message broker is affected. RabbitMQ hasn't been planned to be exposed on the Internet initially; however, a number of security concerns exist even with in-house deployments of the message broker. We will stay away from this fact and not make assumptions on whether the broker instances under consideration are accessible via the Internet or not.

Let's consider again the standard three-cluster diagram (along with an additional remote broker instance) that we have been using so that we can see what security issues may arise in practice:

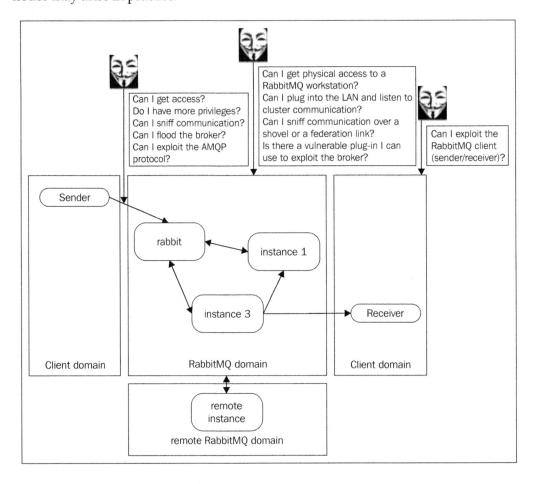

We can apply the following mechanisms in order to mitigate the identified threats:

- **Authentication**: This allows you to identify who connects to the message broker.

- **Authorization**: This allows you to determine the set of privileges and permissions for the authenticated user.

- **Secure communication between the clients and the broker**: By default, messages are exchanged by the senders/receivers and broker instances in an unsecure manner; however, RabbitMQ provides you with a mechanism to establish secure SSL communication.

- **Secure communication between cluster nodes**: Communication between the cluster nodes in the form of Erlang messages is also unsecure, and SSL communication can be established between instance nodes in a RabbitMQ cluster.

- **Secure communication between remote nodes**: As federation links and shovels provide a mechanism to mirror messages across instances over the WAN in a client-server fashion in an unsecure manner, you can establish SSL communication between them as well.

- **Message encryption**: If, by some chance, you cannot reliably secure all the message broker communication channels using SSL, you can encrypt the messages that are sent between the sender and consumer using a proper encryption mechanism (for example, asymmetric encryption with the RSA algorithm using a key of proper length, 2048, 4096, or others). Depending on the mechanism used and performance requirements of the application, there could be a trade-off between security and performance. This applies to the previous cases when SSL communication takes place as well.

- **Proper client settings**: When we discussed performance tuning, we discussed a number of settings for resource utilization of the broker. Many of them can be applied in order to mitigate DoS or DDoS attacks that target resource exhaustion on the message broker by means of sending excessive number of messages, creating a huge number of connections (thus preventing other clients from connecting), or sending an excessive number of AMQP messages.

- **Physical security**: Physical access to the workstations where the message broker is deployed should be properly restricted, and the disks where Mnesia tables reside should be properly encrypted in order to mitigate the risk of data leakage in case of theft (typically, in cases where the message broker stores sensitive data passed through messages).

- **Plugin security**: Plugins can also expose vulnerabilities, so it is important to use plugins from trusted sources that are updated on a regular basis or at least do proper verification that the plugin isn't doing something malicious.

Vulnerability databases such as CVE (Common Vulnerabilities and Exposures) along with other resources on the Internet could prove to be good sources of information regarding known issues against which you can check production deployments of the broker for possible security issues.

In the next sections, we will demonstrate other basic types of attacks and how to get protection against them. Apart from the techniques, we will demonstrate that you need to make sure that you have a message broker upgrade plan set in place. The RabbitMQ team provides security fixes with upcoming releases of the message broker.

Authentication

Let's consider the default setup of a RabbitMQ instance. It comes with a default
`guest` user (with a `guest` password) known by anyone with basic knowledge about
the broker. Moreover, this user has an `administrator` tag giving them full access to
administer the broker, and, even worse, if the RabbitMQ instance port is visible to
the outside world, remote commands can be executed using the `rabbitmqctl` utility
on that workstation using the `eval` command. For this reason, it is advisable (not to
say mandatory) to remove the `guest` user in production deployments. Although the
latest versions of RabbitMQ allow only localhost access for the `guest` user, this still
imposes a high risk for insider attacks. RabbitMQ stores information about users in
an internal database (in the same location where Mnesia stores information about
transient and persistent messages by default). RabbitMQ authentication is provided
by means of the **SASL (Simple Authentication and Security Layer)** framework
that allows the communicating endpoints to negotiate authentication data before
authentication actually takes place. It is defined in the Internet standard RFC 4422.
The following diagram provides a high-level overview of how SASL works in terms
of a sender and the RabbitMQ message broker (note that the diagram is similar for
the message broker and consumer):

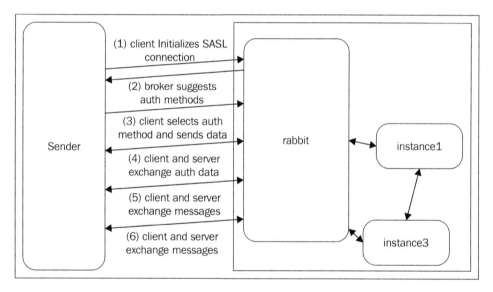

When the client initiates a connection to a RabbitMQ instance, the following things occur:

1. The message broker suggests one or more authentication method to the client. By default, the authentication method suggested by the server and supported by all the clients is PLAIN, which is the most basic type of authentication (equivalent to HTTP basic authentication). RabbitMQ client libraries also provide a mechanism to specify the SASL configuration for the client before trying to establish a connection with the message broker.

2. The client selects one of the methods and sends this information back to the message broker.

3. The client and server start exchanging security information by means of proper handlers depending on the authentication mechanism that is selected. As the SASL framework provides a mechanism for pluggable authentication, each particular authentication mechanism provides a set of server/client handlers to establish and exchange security data. The number of steps in this phase depends on the authentication method.

4. After the authentication mechanism is negotiated and the client is authenticated successfully, the exchange of messages starts taking place. SASL provides a mechanism to establish the confidentiality and integrity of the messages exchanged between the client and server if this is negotiated by them in the previous steps.

When a user is created from the management console, REST API, or the `rabbitadmin` script by default, it is stored as part of the RabbitMQ instance and the information about the user is propagated among the cluster nodes. In practice, however, the instance can be configured to negotiate other types of authentication. If the instance is deployed in an environment where many applications share the same credentials (such as a large enterprise or even a system with multiple components), then the instance may need to use an external service such as an **LDAP (Lightweight Directory Access Protocol)** server or RDBMS for authentication. In this case, you need to make sure that the same SASL configuration is applied among the cluster nodes so that clients that need to reconnect to another cluster node are able to negotiate and authenticate with the same authentication mechanism as the one used when connecting to the original RabbitMQ instance.

In practice, SASL can be implemented in a more general way that allows the client to authenticate the server (in this case, RabbitMQ) but this is not provided out of the box by RabbitMQ (although a plugin with proper support by RabbitMQ clients can provide this support). Currently, the following SASL methods are supported directly (more information is present in the RabbitMQ documentation):

- **PLAIN**: This is the default one
- **AMQPLAIN**: This is the custom version of PLAIN as defined by the AMQP 0-8 standard
- **RABBIT-CR-DEMO**: This is the custom challenge response authentication
- **EXTERNAL**: This is currently supported by means of `rabbitmq_auth_mechanism_ssl` that provides the ability to authenticate a client using the client's public certificate

Configuring the LDAP backend

Let's see, for example, how to move from the default storage of RabbitMQ users to an LDAP server using the OpenLDAP server distribution. First, download OpenLDAP for the operating system of your choice (for Unix-based distribution, you either use the package manager or go to `http://www.openldap.org/`, and for a Windows port, you can go to `http://sourceforge.net/projects/openldapwindows/`). For a Ubuntu-based installation, you need to install the `slapd` and `ldap-utils` packages in order to install OpenLDAP using the following command:

```
sudo apt-get install slapd ldap-utils
```

The Windows installation comes with a convenient installer. After the LDAP server is installed in Windows, you can start the server by running the `<OpenLDAP_install_dir>\libexec\StartLDAP.cmd` script. After the OpenLDAP server is started, navigate to the `<OpenLDAP_install_dir>\sbin` directory and run the following utility in order to set a new root password for the LDAP server (the same configuration applies to the other operating systems):

```
slappasswd.exe
```

You will be prompted to supply a proper root password. After you supply the password twice, you will see it in an encrypted form. Assuming that we have set an example as the root password, you can see the following:

```
{SSHA}VUCblOSqFJn/L9O2bMTrP/YpGDJyAYYx
```

Copy the encrypted password and apply it (the `rootpw` parameter) along with the name of your organization (the `suffix` parameter) and directory root (the `rootdn` parameter) to the `<OpenLDAP_install_dir>\etc\openldap\slapd.conf` OpenLDAP configuration file as follows (modify the already existing parameters):

- `suffix`: dc=example,dc=com

- `rootdn`: cn=organization,dc=example,dc=com

- `rootpw`: {SSHA}VUCblOSqFJn/L9O2bMTrP/YpGDJyAYYx

After the preceding configuration changes have been made, you need to restart the OpenLDAP server. Note that the restart may fail in case there is an `<OpenLDAP_install_dir>\etc\openldap\alock` lock file existing. If this is the case, delete the file and try to start the OpenLDAP server again. Entries in a directory server are organized hierarchically and the mechanisms to add / edit / delete or retrieve them is provided by the LDAP protocol. LDAP and OpenLDAP are huge topics that we will not cover in detail. For now, you can assume that the preceding configuration specifies the root directory for your entries along with the root password used to access this directory. Definitions of the LDAP entries are stored in an `ldiff` file. Using the configured root and password, we will create the following directory structure that has the organization at the root along with a subentry that represents the group of users in the organization and a single user (`Martin`):

The structure is represented by the following `ldiff` file (`sample.ldiff`):

```
# This distinguished name (DN) determines the organization
dn: dc=example,dc=com
objectClass: top
objectClass: dcObject
objectClass: organization
dc: example
o: example
description: Sample description

## Example.com users
dn: ou=users,dc=example,dc=com
ou: users
description: Users in the organization
```

```
objectClass: organizationalUnit

## Sample user
dn: cn=Martin,ou=users,dc=example,dc=com
objectclass: inetOrgPerson
cn: Martin
sn: Toshev
uid: mtoshev
mail: martin@example.com
```

Now, you need to import the element definitions from the `ldiff` file using the `<OpenLDAP_install_dir>\bin\ldapadd` utility as follows:

```
ldapadd -x -D "cn=organization,dc=example,dc=com" -W -f sample.ldiff
```

Note that to delete entries, you can use the `ldapdelete` utility as follows (for example, if you want to remove the last entry that we added):

```
ldapdelete  -D "cn=organization,dc=example,dc=com" "cn= Martin,ou=user
s,dc=example,dc=com" -W
```

RabbitMQ provides you with an LDAP backend by means of the `rabbitmq-auth-backend-ldap` plugin. As the LDAP plugin is already included in the RabbitMQ distribution, you can simply enable it on a node:

```
rabbitmq-plugins enable rabbitmq_auth_backend_ldap
```

After the plugin is enabled, you need to provide proper configuration for the LDAP backend as part of the RabbitMQ configuration. Uncomment the following line in order to enable the backend for a node (remember to apply the same configuration over all the nodes in a cluster):

```
{auth_backends, [rabbit_auth_backend_ldap]}
```

In case you want to fall back to using the standard authentication backend provided by RabbitMQ, you can also add the `rabbit_auth_backend_internal` entry to the list. Add the following under the `rabbitmq_auth_backend_ldap` section to the configuration file:

```
{servers, ["localhost"]},{user_dn_pattern, "cn=${username},ou=users,dc
=example,dc=com"}
{tag_queries, [{administrator, {constant, false}},
{management,     {constant, true}}]}
```

This specifies the hostname (`localhost`) and user **DN** (**Distinguished Name**) pattern; in this case, this is the path of the LDAP entry containing `${username}`, which is replaced by RabbitMQ with the supplied username. Note that there is an alternative mechanism that can bind the username to an arbitrary attribute of the user. Refer to the RabbitMQ LDAP plugin for more details on the alternative configuration. The last section specifies that our users are able to access the management console but they don't have administrative privileges. By default, all LDAP users are non-administrative and are allowed access to the entire broker (all the objects in all `vhosts`). In the next section, we will see how to configure additional permissions for LDAP users when using the plugin (the authorization part of the plugin). Before being able to log in using the preceding user DN pattern, we must set a password for our users. To set a password for the user with the name `Martin` that we created earlier, you can use the `ldappasswd` utility as follows (specify the encrypted form of the example that we used earlier to configure our root LDAP password):

```
ldappasswd -D "cn=organization,dc=example,dc=com" "cn=Martin,ou=users,
dc=example,dc=com" -W -S
```

Now, in order to check whether a user can successfully authenticate, you can take the DN from the RabbitMQ configuration, replace `${username}` with the name of the user (in this case, Martin) that you want to check, and use the `ldapwhoampi` utility as follows:

```
ldapwhoami -vvv -D "cn=Martin,ou=users,dc=example,dc=com" -x -w
example
```

You should see the following if the test succeeds:

```
dn:cn=Martin,ou=users,dc=example,dc=com
Result: Success (0)
```

You should now be able to log in from the management console with the `Martin` user and `example` password. If you omit the `tag_queries` entry from the preceding configuration, you will see a warning similar to the following in the log file when you attempt a login (indicating that the LDAP user is not allowed to access the management console):

```
HTTP access denied: user 'Martin' - Not management user
```

The LDAP plugin provides additional configurations such as SSL support for the LDAP communication; you can refer to the plugin documentation. The authentication backend can be used with other types of SASL authentication such as EXTERNAL, as we will see later in this chapter.

Security considerations

Having configured the proper authentication mechanisms and removing the default user is merely not enough. Simple passwords are easily guessable and a very basic tool can be created based on a RabbitMQ client library that tries to connect to the broker using a list of pregenerated passwords from a proper source that can be used to execute a brute force attack on a RabbitMQ message broker. For this reason, you need to consider the following:

- Setting strong passwords for RabbitMQ users whether they are stored internally in the broker or in an LDAP server.

- Setting a broker threshold on the number of failed login attempts for a RabbitMQ user, which, at the time of writing this, is not supported directly by the message broker unfortunately. However, with some more effort, a good plugin can be contributed that implements a way to configure and enforce password policies.

- Setting SSL communication in order to prevent password sniffing, as we will cover later in this chapter.

- Deploying a proper monitoring solution on the broker workstation that takes into consideration the resource utilization factors that can indicate a security breach, such as increased memory or CPU time consumption.

- Configuring a log auditing tool and storing audit logs for the auditing access. You can further combine the audit logs with a log analyzer that can scan them for possible security breaches. Unfortunately, RabbitMQ does not have such built-in capabilities or plugins; you can either decide to implement a plugin for the purpose or use the utilities provided by the OS (such as **tcpdump** or **iptables** logging rules for Unix-based operating systems) with proper log auditing tools in order to be able to analyze incoming traffic for the message broker.

Authorization

After a client is successfully authenticated by the message broker, it needs to perform some activities in some virtual hosts. In the earlier chapters, we saw that permissions are defined per vhost and live either internally in the message broker or externally. The RabbitMQ LDAP backend plugin that we saw earlier provides you with an ability to store permissions in an LDAP server. The following types of permissions are configured in the message broker:

- **configure**: This allows a resource to be created, modified, or deleted
- **write**: This allows a resource to be written to
- **read**: This allows a resource to be read from

We already discussed how to manage permissions using the `rabbitmqctl` utility and the HTTP API. The following commands can be used from the utility to manage permissions:

- `set_permissions`: This sets permissions per user per vhost
- `clear_permissions`: This clears permissions per user per vhost
- `list_permissions`: This lists the users that are granted access to a particular vhost along with their permissions
- `list_user_permissions`: This lists the permissions of a particular user

LDAP authentication

The LDAP user that we created earlier by default has all the permissions to the broker (except for being an administrator). Let's suppose that we want to disable the `configure` permissions, allow more fine-grained `write` permissions only to certain queues (in certain vhosts), or make it an administrator. The RabbitMQ LDAP provides a query mechanism to check permissions as configured in the LDAP server. There are three types of queries that can be specified in the RabbitMQ configuration and further contain different types of subqueries that are executed against the LDAP server:

- `vhost_access_query`: As users and permissions must be checked against vhosts that must be created in RabbitMQ, we can define vhost entries in the LDAP server against which to check for available permissions and tags. In fact, these entries represent a subset of the existing vhosts in the RabbitMQ server against which we check whether users have further access permissions or not. The default query is {`constant`, `true`}, which specifies that access to all vhosts is given to all the users (the `constant` queries are aliases for all, which return true or false for any value checked by `vhost_access_query`).

- `resource_access_query`: These are the types of queries that allow you to check whether a user has specific permissions (read, write, or configure) for a particular vhost to which the user has access (as checked by `vhost_access_query`). The default is {`constant`, `true`}.

- `tag_queries`: These are the types of queries that allow you to specify the tags that are given to particular users (such as **management** or **administrator**). The default is {`administrator`, {`constant`, `false`}}.

The types of subqueries that can be specified for each type of these queries use a simple DSL; you can review the LDAP RabbitMQ plugin documentation for an extensive list of all types of subqueries. We will specify the following access domains for our message broker:

- The `test` user is the vhost
- The `guest` user is an administrator and has access to the management console
- The `Martin` user has access only to the `test` vhost and can publish to exchanges starting with the `test_` prefix
- The `Subscriber` user has access to the `test` vhost only and can read messages from queues starting with the `test_` prefix

The following diagram specifies the LDAP structure of the organization:

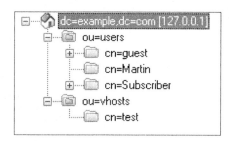

Before we can implement this setup, we need to create the test vhost in RabbitMQ. The following example creates the test vhost using the `rabbitmqctl` utility:

```
rabbitmqctl add_vhost test
```

You also need to create LDAP entries for the `guest` and `Subsciber` users in the same manner that we created the entry for the user with the name Martin earlier. Here is a sample `ldiff` file (`users.ldiff`) for the two users:

```
## guest user
dn: cn=guest,ou=users,dc=example,dc=com
objectclass: inetOrgPerson
cn: guest
sn: guest
uid: guest
mail: guest@example.com

## Subscriber user
dn: cn=Subscriber,ou=users,dc=example,dc=com
objectclass: inetOrgPerson
cn: Subscriber
```

```
sn: Subscriber
uid: Subscriber
mail: subscriber@example.com
```

To import the preceding ldiff file and set a password for the users, you can execute the following set of commands:

```
ldapadd -x -D "cn=organization,dc=example,dc=com" -W -f
users.ldiff
ldappasswd -D "cn=organization,dc=example,dc=com" "cn=guest,ou=users,d
c=example,dc=com" -W -S
ldappasswd -D "cn=organization,dc=example,dc=com" "cn=Subscriber,ou=us
ers,dc=example,dc=com" -W -S
```

Finally, we need to create the `vhosts` group along with an entry for the `test` vhost (`vhosts.ldiff`):

```
## Example.com vhosts
dn: ou=vhosts,dc=example,dc=com
ou: vhosts
description: Vhosts in the organization
objectClass: organizationalUnit

## test vhost
dn: cn=test,ou=vhosts,dc=example,dc=com
objectclass: organizationalRole
description: test vhost
```

Execute the following in order to import the preceding entries:

```
ldapadd -x -D "cn=organization,dc=example,dc=com" -W -f vhosts.ldiff
```

Note that we are using a predefined object class (`organizationalRole`) for the vhost entry in LDAP. You can prefer to create your own object class for the purpose of describing a vhost along with its attributes in your organization. Finally, we need to specify the proper queries for permission checking in the LDAP configuration (as part of the `rabbitmq_auth_backend_ldap` section in your RabbitMQ configuration file):

```
{vhost_access_query,      {exists,
                              "cn=${vhost},ou=vhosts,dc=example,dc=com"}},
{resource_access_query,
   {for, [
   {permission, configure, {match,
{string, "${username}"},{string, "guest"}}},
   {permission, write, {'and', [
```

```
{match, {string, "${username}"},
        {string, "(Martin|guest"}},
{match, {string, "${name}"},{string, "test_*"}}]} },
{permission, read, {'and', [
{match, {string, "${username}"},
        {string, "(Subscriber|guest)"}},
{match, {string, "${name}"},{string, "test_*"}}]} }
] }},
{tag_queries, [{administrator,
              {match, {string, "${username}"},
              {string, "guest"}}},
          {management,   {constant, true}}]}
```

The preceding configuration is easy to understand, but it might turn out to be clumsy to write and test. After it is added to the configuration file, you can try to log in with the guest/guest user and check whether it has administrative access. You can try to create an object using the `Subscriber` user or send/receive messages using the `Martin`/`Subscriber` user. In practice, the preceding configuration should be designed carefully based on the organizational LDAP schema in order to prevent security holes.

Secure communication

Let's turn our attention to how the AMQP messages can be transferred securely on the wire and how to ensure secure communication between the publishers/subscribers and our message broker. Even if the message broker is not visible to the outside world, there is still the risk of an insider attack taking place. This could be either a network tap or hub that is added with malicious intent to the communication link between the message broker and publishing/subscribing applications or a form of ARP (address resolution protocol) poisoning. In both cases, traffic can be forwarded to a listening port on a machine that aims to sniff communication. The next step is to capture and analyze the incoming traffic. To simulate the capturing and analysis phase, we will use Wireshark (version.1.12.8) along with the AMQP dissector module that comes with the tool in order to listen on the network interface of a local workstation that has a RabbitMQ instance running. First, download and install Wireshark from `https://www.wireshark.org/`. As we will be listening for traffic on the loopback interface, you need to make sure that you have proper support to listen on the loopback interface in your OS. For Windows, WireShark uses the WinPcap utility that, at the time of writing this, does not support listening on the loopback interface. The Npcap tool is an update of WinPcap that provides a generic loopback interface for Windows (check `https://wiki.wireshark.org/CaptureSetup/Loopback` in the Wireshark, *Wikipedia*). Download and install Npcap if you are using Wireshark and RabbitMQ under Windows.

Once WireShark is installed, navigate to **Capture -> Interfaces...**, and select the network interface on which you will listen for the incoming traffic, as shown in the following screenshot:

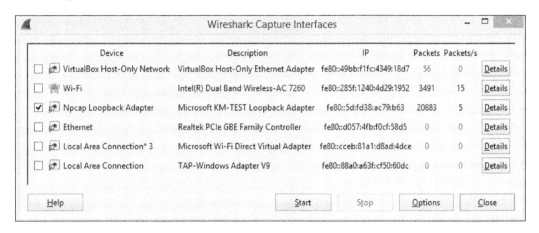

Then, click on **Close** in the **Filter** field, specify amqp as a display filter, and select **Capture >- Start** in order to start the capturing of packets on the loopback interface. Send a test message to the RabbitMQ broker (you can use a modified version of the RequestSenderDemo Java class introduced in *Chapter 3, Administration, configuration and management* for this purpose) using test_exchange with the test_queue key on the test vhost (precreate the test_exchange exchange and the test_queue queue). The result from the capture is visible on the following screen:

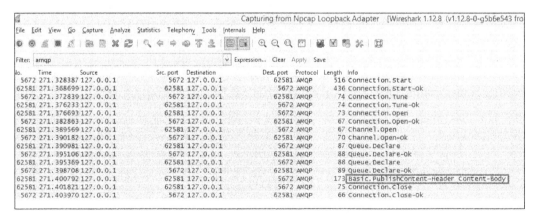

You can see the entire sequence of AMQP messages that are exchanged when the message was sent. If you double-click on the **Basic Publish** package (in the rectangle) and scroll down a little, you will see the message payload:

As you can see, it was pretty straightforward to inspect the unsecured RabbitMQ traffic once you are able to receive the network traffic to/from the message broker. In order to deal with the problem, we need to enable SSL in the RabbitMQ configuration. In order to listen for the SSL connection, the RabbitMQ message broker needs to specify a port for the SSL connection along with the additional SSL options such as CA certificate file, server certificate, and private key, and also needs to specify whether to verify the client certificate (if any) and not and how to behave if verification fails (accept or reject the client connection). The following sample configuration enables SSL support on a RabbitMQ instance on port 5671:

```
[
  {rabbit, [
    {ssl_listeners, [5671]},
    {ssl_options, [{cacertfile,"cacert.pem"},
                   {certfile,"cert.pem"},
                   {keyfile,"key.pem"},
                   {verify, verify_peer},
                   {fail_if_no_peer_cert,true}]}
  ]}
].
```

The preceding configuration further specifies that the client must also send its certificate and that it must be verified by the message broker. Apart from setting the port to 5671 in the client connection factory, you must also tell the client to use SSL when connecting to the broker. The following example prepares the connecting factory in the Java client before creating SSL connections to the message broker:

```
ConnectionFactory factory = new ConnectionFactory();
factory.setHost("localhost");
factory.setPort(5671);
factory.useSslProtocol();
```

In this case, the client does not present a certificate to the broker and does not validate the broker's certificate. To do so, you can supply a `javax.net.sslSSLContext` instance that contains a key store with the client certificate and trust store with the server certificate to the `useSslProtocl()` method. The RabbitMQ documentation provides a detailed example on how to create your own certificate authority, generate keys and server certificates, and sign the server certificate by the CA—the OpenSSL tool is used to perform these activities. Check the RabbitMQ SSL guide for more details:

```
https://www.rabbitmq.com/ssl.html
```

Secure communication with the management interface

If the management interface port (15672 by default) is not restricted by a firewall rule, then SSL must be enabled for the management plugin as well. Let's use Wireshark again to demonstrate what can happen if the administrator forgets to restrict access to the management interface or does not enable SSL. Start capturing packets from Wireshark, and in the **Filter** field, specify a display filter that permits only packets to/from the TCP port 15672 using the following expression:

```
tcp.port eq 15672
```

Now, send a test message to the management interface REST API using the `rabbitmqadmin` utility:

```
rabbitmqadmin.py -V test publish routing_key=test_queue
exchange=test_exchange payload=test
```

The following diagram observes the captured traffic flowing to/from the management interface:

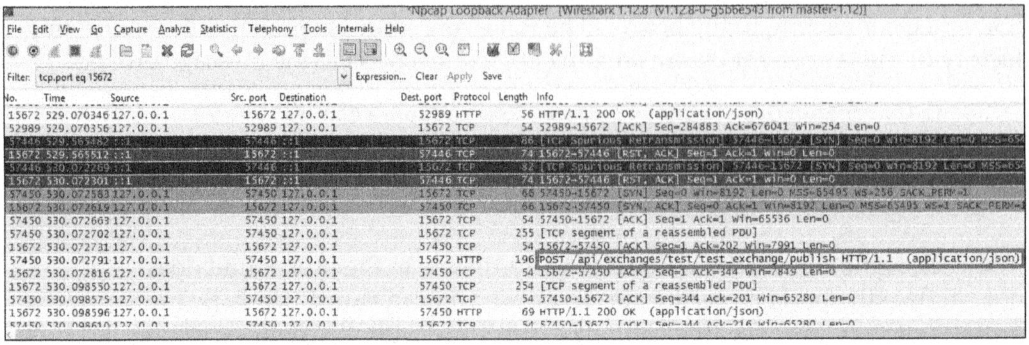

In the red rectangle, you can see the HTTP packet that sends a POST request with the message to the management interface. If you click on the packet and scroll down a little, you will see the information about the AMQP message along with the payload:

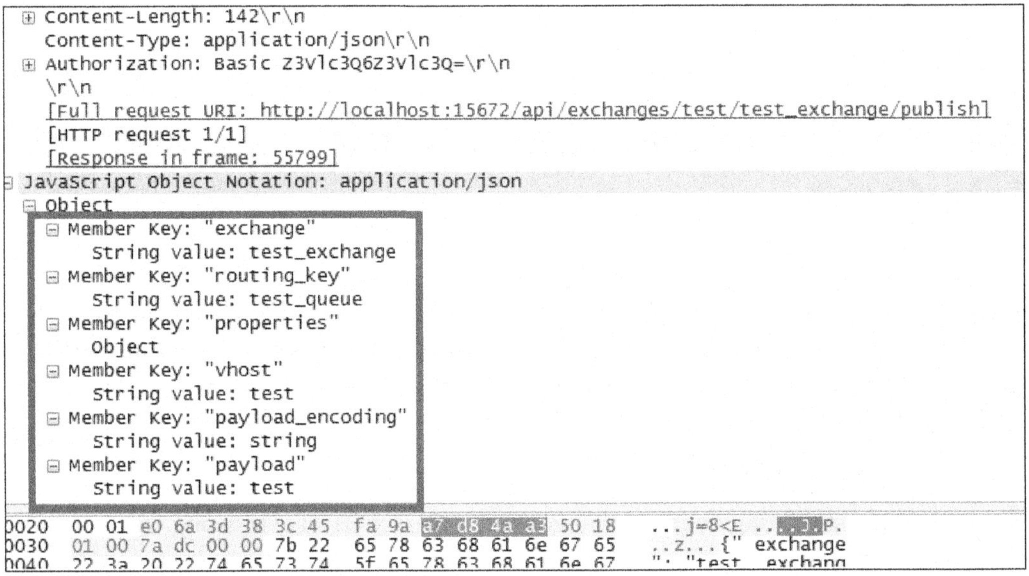

In order to enable SSL for the management interface, you must change its configuration. The following example provides a sample configuration that enables SSL on port 15671:

```
[{rabbitmq_management,
    [{listener, [{port,      15671},
                 {ssl,       true},
```

```
                {ssl_opts, [{cacertfile, "cacert.pem"},
                            {certfile,   "cert.pem"},
                            {keyfile,    "key.pem"}]}
            ]}
    ]}
  ].
```

As you can see, the configuration is very similar to the one that we specified for the enabling of an SSL for a connection to the message broker.

Secure cluster communication

Although an Erlang cookie is used to allow communication between nodes in a cluster, it still doesn't enable secure communication between these nodes. To do so, you need to enable SSL in the Erlang application that runs the RabbitMQ instance. For further details on how to enable SSL communication between nodes, you can check the clustering SSL guide from the RabbitMQ documentation:

http://www.erlang.org/doc/apps/ssl/ssl_distribution.html

Apart from setting secure clustering, you must also ensure that filesystem access to the Erlang cookie is given only to users who are allowed to run and manage the RabbitMQ instance on that system.

EXTERNAL SSL authentication

The rabbitmq-auth-mechanism-ssl context provides an SASL EXTERNAL type of authentication that uses a client certificate to authenticate a user. The plugin requires SSL communication to be enabled between the client and RabbitMQ server. For more details about the configuration of the plugin, you can check the plugin repository at https://github.com/rabbitmq/rabbitmq-auth-mechanism-ssl.

Penetration testing

Now that we have seen how to secure our message broker, we also need to test that our setup is indeed in place and really prevents attackers from bringing down the message broker or stealing messages. For this reason, you can build your own custom tool for penetration testing of the message broker, which performs the following functions:

- It checks whether the guest/guest user is present and it can perform administrative activities.

- It tries to brute-force passwords for an existing set of users, either based on a password generation policy or using a predefined password database.

- It tries to access prohibited vhosts from a particular set of users.

- It uses nmap to check whether the management console and RabbitMQ communication ports are visible; this step may include checks on ports that are exposed by RabbitMQ plugins.

- It checks the RabbitMQ configuration settings, authentication mechanism, and currently-set limits such as minimum free disk space, memory limits, or maximum number of channels. (Most of these options were covered when we discussed the performance tuning of the message broker.)

- It checks the maximum limit per user as specified by the operating system, for example, this could be the maximum number of processes or file descriptors that can be used for the user that runs the RabbitMQ instance. In Linux, this could be checked against the `etc/security/limits.conf` file.

More features can be derived from the following article that covers several security considerations and resource utilization settings for production deployments of RabbitMQ:

```
https://www.rabbitmq.com/production-checklist.html
```

Case study – securing CSN

Once the CSN was in alpha testing and the good performance of the system was reached, the CSN team was required to take two important steps in order to meet the company's security policy:

- Enable SSL over all the communication links between all the components in the system (including the RabbitMQ cluster links, federation link with the remote RabbitMQ instance, and communication links between the broker and its clients)

- Enable the central management of CSN users and their associated permissions by means of the corporate LDAP server

Further security testing was made by the team in order to ensure that no major vulnerabilities were found in the setup of the system:

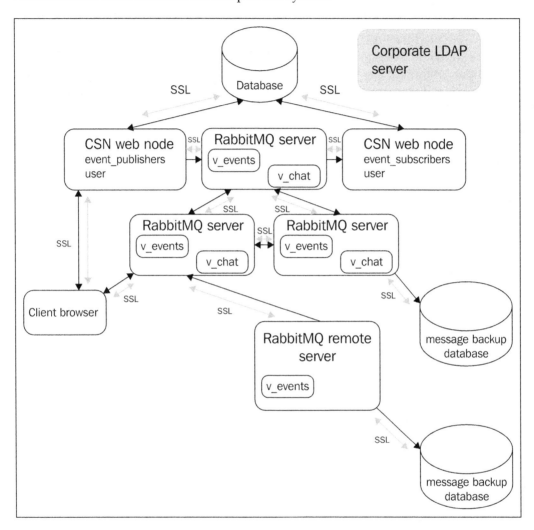

Summary

In this chapter, we discussed the various aspects of security related to RabbitMQ and the types of vulnerabilities that can come up in practice and how to mitigate them. We covered the SASL mechanism provided by RabbitMQ for the purpose of authentication and extended further on this concept by providing an integration of the authentication backend with the OpenLDAP server. Additionally, we discussed how to store and manage permissions in LDAP and provide secure communication with the message broker, management console, and cluster nodes. In the end, we covered several guidelines in establishing a successful penetration testing strategy to verify that the message broker meets the minimum level of security as required by the policy of your organization.

Exercises

1. What types of security threats are imposed on the message broker?
2. What is SASL, and what types of SASL authentication are supported in RabbitMQ?
3. How does RabbitMQ enable authentication and authorization against an LDAP server?
4. How does RabbitMQ provide SSL support?
5. How can you test whether your RabbitMQ setup provides a good degree of security?

10
Internals

To get a better understanding of how a system works, on various occasions, developers need to dig under the hood in the implementation of that system or at least get a basic overview of its high-level architecture and its most critical components. In this chapter, we will discuss how RabbitMQ is designed and implemented and how to write plugins for RabbitMQ.

The topics that will be covered in the chapter are as follows:

- High-level architecture for RabbitMQ
- Overview of RabbitMQ components
- Developing plugins for RabbitMQ

High level architecture of RabbitMQ

We already discussed a lot of details about how the message broker works. We discussed that RabbitMQ instances are Erlang applications that communicate with each other by means of Erlang message passing with the help of a shared Erlang cookie that is used to allow communication between endpoints. As every system that provides a server and one or more clients for different platforms, we could easily guess that before an AMQP message is sent to the broker, an AMQP client opens a TCP socket using the utilities that are provided by the particular programming language in which it writes the AMQP data. The most interesting part is what happens when the message arrives at the message broker. Once the message broker receives the AMQP message, it needs to parse and process it, accordingly. If we take a closer look at what the `rabbitmq-server` script executes, we will notice that several actions take place, as follows:

- The `start` method from the `rabbit_prelaunch` module is executed and it performs the basic validation (such as, whether a node with the same name exists and whether the node distribution port is valid) before actually starting the server.

If the checks from the previous step are successful, then the server starts from the `rabbit` module that implements the `application` behavior (meaning that the module has certain callback methods that must be implemented by the module).

Before we are to understand how RabbitMQ works, we need to clarify a few important features provided by Erlang and their uses in the implementation of the message broker. A `behaviour`, in terms of the Erlang programming language, specifies that a module must implement certain methods that give it a certain meaning (behavior). We can compare this with the way in which inheritance works—we can have an abstract class that extracts certain logic and can be extended by different implementations, which on the other hand, can be further extended. In that sense, an Erlang module can either define that it has a certain behavior (and it needs to implement a particular set of callback methods that are defined by that behavior) or the module itself is a behavior that defines a set of methods that must be implemented by other modules that use the behavior. In the following example, we have a sample module that uses the built-in application behavior and defines the sample behavior with two functions: `start_sender` and `start_receiver`, as follows:

```
-module(sample).
-export([behaviour_info/1]).
-behaviour(application).
start(normal, []) -> true.
behaviour_info(callbacks) ->
    [{start_sender,2},
     {start_receiver, 0}
];
```

The `sample` module uses the application behavior and needs to provide the implementation of the `start(normal, [])` method that is executed before the application (this module) is started successfully. On the other hand, the module creates a behavior with the same name as that of the module using the `behaviour_info` method that specifies the callback functions along with their arity (number of arguments) that must be implemented by the users of the `sample` behavior. This seemingly simple mechanism lays the basis for creating more complex interactions among the components of an Erlang application. Two of these mechanisms are built in Erlang and used by RabbitMQ, as shown in the following:

- The `supervisor` behavior allows the creation of a process tree. The main purpose of this behavior is to allow a parent process to monitor the child processes for failure and restart them, based on a predefined policy in that parent (supervisor) process. This allows a fault-tolerant handling of the failures in the application, which is necessary in the case of RabbitMQ in order to ensure a decent degree of reliability that prevents the broker from failing upon process failure.

- The gen_event behavior allows the exchange of messages between processes.

The supervisor behavior is essential for Erlang and for the RabbitMQ message broker, in particular. A good understanding of how and why RabbitMQ relies on a supervision tree of processes is necessary in order to understand how the message broker works at the runtime. Consider the following diagram that provides an overview of a sample process tree in terms of Erlang and the supervisor behavior:

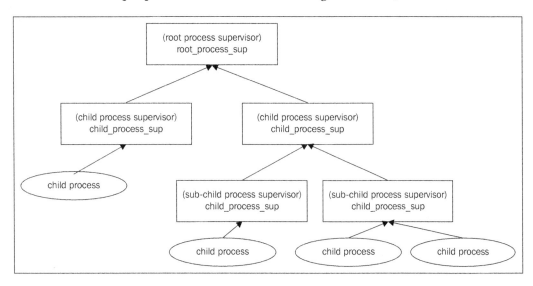

We have a root process that supervises other processes; if any of them fail, the supervisor is responsible to restart it. The leaves of the tree are the actual processes that are running in the application.

The following diagram provides a high-level overview of the RabbitMQ components and their initialization during the server startup:

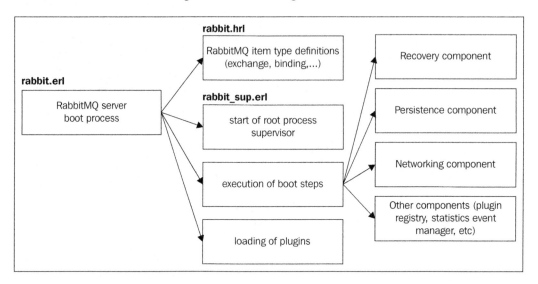

The `rabbit` module uses the `rabbit.hrl` Erlang header file that provides the definitions of all types (such as, queue, exchange, binding, vhost, and so on) that are used in the server and for this reason, the header is included in most of the Erlang sources of the message broker. The `start(normal, [])` method of the `rabbit` module triggers the start up of the server. First, the root process supervisor that is provided by the `rabbit_sup` module is started by invoking the `rabbit_sup:start_link()` method. Then, a number of boot steps are executed (we will refer to this process as the boot component of the message broker). Many of the boot steps start a child process, which is added to the supervisor tree that has a certain role. The following diagram describes the process tree, one level under the `rabbit_sup` supervisor:

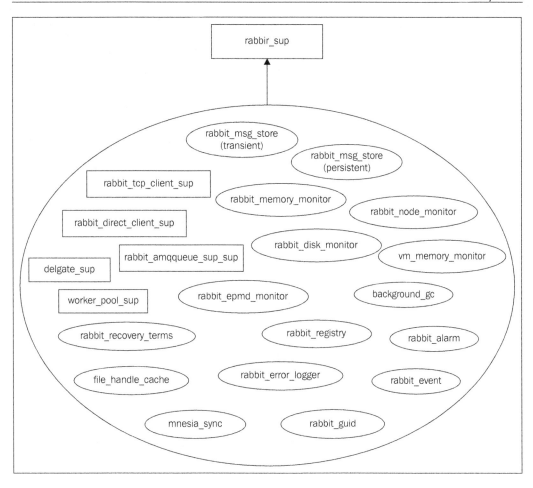

In the next section, we will briefly discuss most of the processes that are mentioned in the preceding diagram, along with the structure of the process subtrees that are provided by the most essential child supervisors, such as `rabbit_tcp_client_sup`, `rabbit_direct_client_sup`, and `rabbit_amqqueue_sup_sup`, and their corresponding Erlang modules. Apart from when networking is started as a part of the boot process on or more `tcp_listener_sup` supervisor processes are started for each TCP/SSL interface configured for the message broker.

After the boot steps are finished, the RabbitMQ plugins are loaded. At this point, the message broker is ready to accept the connections. Logging in the RabbitMQ components is done by means of the utilities provided by the `rabbit_log` module.

Overview of RabbitMQ components

Before we dive into more details on the separate components of the message broker and their implementation, you can refer to *Appendix A, Contributing to RabbitMQ* on how to get the RabbitMQ source code so that you can review it as we move through the components and also how to install useful tools that will aid in Erlang development and RabbitMQ plugin development, in particular.

Boot component

The RabbitMQ boot component provides one of the key mechanisms in the message broker that allows the plugins to require certain steps from the RabbitMQ server in order to ensure that the components that they depend on are already loaded and it also allows the plugins to be installed and enabled in the RabbitMQ message broker. For this reason, it is advisable to write plugins with caution as they can crash the message broker if they are not implemented properly. Before the RabbitMQ boot mechanism is triggered, the common `rabbit_sup` process supervisor (the root of the RabbitMQ process tree) is started by calling the `rabbit_sup:start_link()` method from the `start/2` method in the `rabbit` module. After the process supervisor starts, a series of boot steps are executed by calling the `rabbit_boot_steps:run_boot_steps()` method. The boot steps are divided into groups, as follows:

- `external_infrastructure`: This prepares the infrastructure for the RabbitMQ server (such as, worker pool, file handle cache, and Mnesia database)

- `kernel_ready`: This initializes the core functionality of the message broker (such as plug-in registry, message logging, and statistics collection)

- `core_intialized`: This initializes the additional functions of the message broker (such as memory alarms, distribution of messages among queues, cluster node notifications, and memory monitoring)

- `routing_ready`: This initializes more startup activities (such as recovery of queues, exchanges and bindings, and initialization of queue mirrors)

- `final steps`: This performs the final startup activities (such as error log initialization, initialization of TCP listeners for configured interfaces, initialization of processes that are used to handle client connection, and sending of notifications to join the current RabbitMQ cluster)

The steps are organized in a directed acyclic graph and each step may specify predecessor steps that may be executed first and successor steps that might be execute after the current step. For example, the following boot step is used to add mirrors to the queues based on the mirroring policies that are defined in the message broker:

```
-rabbit_boot_step({mirrored_queues,
                  [{description, "adding mirrors to queues"},
                   {mfa, {rabbit_mirror_queue_misc, on_node_up, []}},
                   {requires, recovery},
                   {enables, routing_ready}]}).
```

It requires the recovery step to be executed beforehand and enables the execution of the routing_ready step. The routing_ready step represents a group (and all other groups that are mentioned earlier are represented as steps):

```
-rabbit_boot_step({routing_ready,
                  [{description, "message delivery logic ready"},
                   {requires, core_initialized}]}).
```

Each group step represents a barrier for the execution of steps from the next group. In the preceding example, the routing_ready group requires the core_initialized step to have been completed (and the core_initialized step will finish after all the steps that enable the core_initialized have finished executing).

The sequence of steps that are executed during the boot process is as follows:

- The external_infrastructure group steps are as follow:
  - codec_correctness_check: This checks whether the AMQP binary generator is working correctly and is able to generate the correct AMQP frames.
  - rabbit_alarm: This enables the RabbitMQ alarm handlers (disk and memory); when the memory grows beyond a threshold or disk space drops below a limit, alarms are triggered in order to notify the broker that it must block subsequent connections to the broker.
  - database: This prepares the Mnesia database.
  - database_sync: This starts the mnesia_sync process.
  - file_handle_cache: This handles file read/write synchronization.
  - worker_pool: This provides a mechanism to limit the maximum parallelism for a job (jobs can be executed synchronously or asynchronously). It is used for some operations in the message broker, such as executing transactions in the Mnesia database.

- The `kernel_ready` group steps are shown in the following:
  - ° `rabbit_registry`: This starts a registry that stores the plugin information along with the corresponding Erlang modules for the registered plugins.
  - ° `rabbit_event`: This starts the event notifications process that is used for the statistics collection.

- The following are the `core_initialized` group steps:
  - ° `rabbit_memory_monitor`: This starts the `rabbit_memory_monitor` process.
  - ° `guid_generator`: This starts the `rabbit_guid` process that provides a service for the generation of unique random numbers across the RabbitMQ service instance that is used for various purposes (such as use in autogenerated queue names).
  - ° `delegate_sup`: This starts a process manager that is used to spread the tasks among child processes (for example, to send a message from an exchange to one or more queues).
  - ° `rabbit_node_monitor`: This starts the `rabbit_node_monitor` process.
  - ° `rabbit_epmd_monitor`: This starts the `rabbit_epmd_monitor` process.

- The `routing_ready` group steps are as follows:
  - ° `empty_db_check`: This verifies that the Mnesia database runs fine and if necessary, inserts the default database data (such as guest/guest user and default vhost).
  - ° `recovery`: This recovers the bindings between exchanges and queues and starts the queues.
  - ° `mirrored_queues`: This adds mirrors to queues, as defined by the mirroring policies.

- The following are the final boot steps:
  - ° `log_relay step`: This starts the `rabbit_error_logger` process.
  - ° `direct_client`: This starts the supervisor tree that takes care of accepting direct client connections.
  - ° `networking`: This starts up the `tcp_listener_sup` handlers for each combination of TCP interface/port that will accept incoming connections for the message broker.
  - ° `notify_cluster`: This notifies the current cluster that a node is started.
  - ° `background_gc`: This starts the `background_gc` process that provides a service to force garbage collection on demand.

As additional reading on the boot process of RabbitMQ, the entries from the following GitHub repository at `https://github.com/videlalvaro/rabbit-internals` can be reviewed.

Plug-in loader component

Plugin's loading is triggered by the `broker_start()` method in the `rabbit` module once the boot steps of the message broker has finished executing. To recall briefly, the following table lists the configuration properties that are related to RabbitMQ plugins:

RABBITMQ_PLUGINS_DIR	The directory where RabbitMQ plugins are found
RABBITMQ_PLUGINS_EXPAND_DIR	The directory where the enabled RabbitMQ plugins are expanded before starting the messaging server
RABBITMQ_ENABLED_PLUGINS_FILE	The location of the file that specifies which plugins are enabled

The `start()` method of the `rabbit_plugins` module is called and it clears the plugins expand directory, reads a list of the enabled plugins from the enabled plugins file, reads the location of the RabbitMQ plugin directory, builds a dependency graph from the list of all the plugins in that directory from where the enabled plugins and their dependencies are retrieved, and finally, they are unzipped to the plugins expand directory. The `start_apps()` method that uses the `app_utils` module is then called in order to load the plugins; the application module (module that implements the `application` behavior) of each plugin is loaded and the `start()` method of the plugins application is called.

Recovery component

For the recovery component, we will understand two particular steps from the boot process, as follows:

1. **queue, exchange and binding recovery**: This is provided by the retrieves information about the items from Mnesia such as durable queues and exchanges along with the bindings between them and starts the queues. For this purpose, the `recover()` method from the `rabbit_policy`, `rabbit_amqqueue`, `rabbit_binding`, and `rabbit_exchange` modules are used. The `rabbit_amqqueue` module recovers queues by first retrieving durable queues from the Mnesia database. Then, two processes for transient and persistent message storing (represented by the `rabbit_msg_store` module) are started and bound to the `rabbit_sup` supervisor process (this is done by calling the `start()` method from the `rabbit_variable_queue` default backing module). After this, a queue supervisor of all the queue-related supervisors from the `rabbit_amqqueue_sup_sup` module is started. Finally, the durable queues are recovered by starting a `rabbit_amqqueue_sup` queue supervisor process for each queue (from the `rabbit_amqqueue_sup_sup` supervisor, which specifies the child specification for the child processes in its `init()` method). Each queue supervisor process starts one queue process (represented by the `rabbit_amqqueue_process` module) and one queue slave process for queue mirroring (represented by the `rabbit_mirror_queue_slave` module). Once the recovery is completed, the `start()` method from the `rabbit_amqqueue` module is invoked, which triggers the `go()` method in `rabbit_mirror_queue_slave` that further invokes (via the `gen_server2` module RPC) the `handle_go()` method. This joins the queue slave process for the particular queue to a group of processes in order to distribute information in a broadcast manner among these processes. This broadcast mechanism is implemented by the `gm` module (which stands for guaranteed broadcast) that provides the necessary utilities to add/remove a process from a broadcast group and send a broadcast message among nodes in a group in a reliable manner.

2. Start up of queue mirroring based on the mirroring policies defined for the recovered queues. For this purpose, the `on_node_up()` method from the `rabbit_mirror_queue_misc` module is executed. It retrieves the cluster nodes on which to mirror queue messages for each queue based on the defined mirroring policies. The `rabbit_mirror_*` modules implement the logic for queue mirroring using master-slave semantics.

The following diagram depicts the process subtree for the queue-related processes and their supervisors:

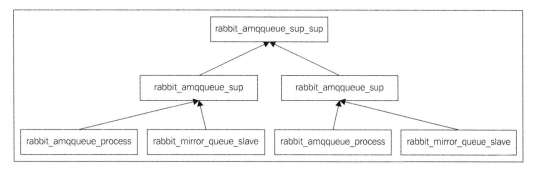

Persistence component

We will divide the persistence component into metadata persistence and message persistence subcomponents.

Metadata persistence

In the boot process, we have a chain for the initialization of the Mnesia databases along with the relevant RabbitMQ tables. In earlier chapters, we discussed that the transient and persistent message stores are separated from the Mnesia tables, which store the information about object definitions (such as exchanges, queues, and bindings). The `rabbit_mnesia` module is initialized during the boot process and provides utilities to start and stop the Mnesia database, check whether the database is running, and transfer metadata among cluster nodes. It also handles the creation of the Mnesia schema along with the RabbitMQ tables by means of the `rabbit_table` module. The `rabbit_table` module provides definitions of the RabbitMQ tables. The following is a list of the RabbitMQ Mnesia tables:

- `rabbit_user`
- `rabbit_user_permission`
- `rabbit_vhost`
- `rabbit_listener`
- `rabbit_durable_route`
- `rabbit_semi_durable_route`
- `rabbit_route,`
- `rabbit_reverse_route`

- `rabbit_topic_trie_node`
- `rabbit_topic_trie_edge`
- `rabbit_topic_trie_binding`
- `rabbit_durable_exchange`
- `rabbit_exchange`
- `rabbit_exchange_serial`
- `exchange_name_match`
- `rabbit_runtime_parameters`
- `rabbit_durable_queue`
- `rabbit_queue`

The preceding tables are manipulated by means of the `mnesia` built in the module throughout the RabbitMQ server sources. The `rabbit_mnesia` module uses the file utilities that are provided by the `rabbit_file` module.

Message persistence component

First of all, the file handle cache is initialized by the `start_fhc()` method in the rabbit module. The file handle cache provides a buffer for read/write operations on the disk that manages the available file descriptors among processes that use the file handle cache (readers/writers). You can think of the file handle cache as a service that accepts jobs for read/write operations by means of the `with_handle()` methods, which accept a function closure providing the execution logic for a file operation and serves as a guard to acquire/release the file handles in order to accomplish that operation. The `rabbit_file` module uses `file_handle_cache` to perform disk operations. In the RabbitMQ configuration file, we can specify a `backing_queue_module` setting, which specifies an Erlang module that provides the queue operations, such as initialization and management of the message store, message processing in the queue (in-memory or on disk), queue purging, and so on. The default implementation is provided by the `rabbit_variable_queue` module that uses `rabbit_msg_store` to store transient and persistent messages on the disk. To do so, `rabbit_msg_store` uses the utilities that are provided by the `rabbit_file` and `file_handle_cache` modules.

Networking component

The networking component is initialized during the boot process by calling the
`boot()` method from the `rabbit_direct` and `rabbit_networking` modules. The
first module starts the `rabbit_direct_client_sup` supervisor process to handle
direct connections to the broker, while the second module starts `rabbit_tcp_`
`client_sup` to handle the TCP client connections. The `rabbit_tcp_client_sup`
also creates a `rabbit_connection_sup` supervisor that, on the other hand, creates
a `rabbit_reader` process to process the connections and a `helper_sup` process
(represented by the `rabbit_connection_helper_sup` module) to create channel
supervisors. After that, a TCP listener supervisor is started for each TCP/SSL listener
interface. For each TCP/SSL listener supervisor, two child processes are created
(their specifications are provided in the `init()` method of the `rabbit_listener_`
`sup` method), as follows:

- A `tcp_listener` process that accepts connections on a specified port
- A `tcp_acceptor_sup` process that creates a number of child acceptor
  processing to handle incoming socket connections from the `tcp_listener`
  process

The following diagram provides an overview of the interaction between the
processes that are involved in accepting and processing a TCP connection in the
message broker over a single interface:

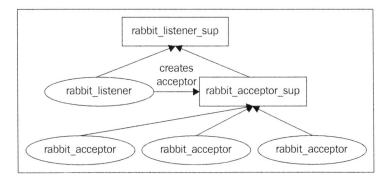

Once an acceptor receives a client connections, it calls the `start_client()` method for TCP connections or the `start_ssl_client()` method for SSL connections from the `rabbit_networking` module to process the incoming connection. The new connection is sent to the `rabbit_reader` process that starts reading the AMQP messages from the connection. It also provides the semantics to parse the messages and create channel-level processes by means of the `helper_sup` process. The following diagram provides an overview of the process subtree, originating from the `rabbit_tcp_client_sup` supervisor:

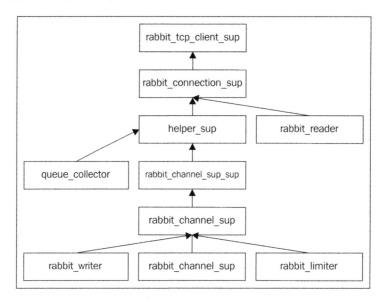

Other components

There are other components provided by the message broker; we briefly covered most of them when we were discussing the boot process of the message broker. In short, these components include the following:

- Alarm handler module that triggers memory alarms in case of excessive memory consumption; its implementation is provided by the `rabbit_alarm` module.

- RabbitMQ plugin registry that provides a service to register plugin modules to the message broker and retrieve information about the plugin modules from the various components of the broker; its implementation is provided by the `rabbit_registry` module.

- Statistics event manager that enables gathering of statistics from the message broker; its implementation is provided by the `rabbit_event` module.

- Node monitoring provides a mechanism to monitor addition and removal of nodes from a cluster and also track the current cluster status; its implementation is provided by the `rabbit_node_monitor` module.

- Memory monitoring provides a mechanism for central collection of statistics that are related to memory consumption in the broker; each queue sends information to the memory monitor upon changes in the queue contents. This allows the memory monitor to track the statistics about the overall memory consumption; its implementation is provided by the `rabbit_memory_monitor` module.

- Custom garbage collection process allows components to force Erlang garbage collection for processes that are running in the message broker. garbage collection, in particular, is forced when a memory alarm is triggered; its implementation is provided by the `background_gc` module.

Developing plug-ins for RabbitMQ

Having seen how the message broker works, it is time to see how to write a plugin for RabbitMQ. It should be stressed again that a poorly written plugin can result in the crashing of the entire broker, therefore, you should be careful when implementing a plugin for the message broker that is intended to be used in production.

There is a public umbrella project that can be used as a starting point in writing a new RabbitMQ plugin. The umbrella project groups a number of sample child projects, which implement different types of plugins that you can use as an example. Refer to *Appendix, Contributing to RabbitMQ* on tools for Erlang development. In order to get the project from the RabbitMQ repository and check the child projects, execute the following set of commands:

```
git clone https://github.com/rabbitmq/rabbitmq-public-umbrella.git
cd rabbitmq-public-umbrella
make co
```

The `rabbitmq_metronome` can be used as a starting point as it provides a very basic functionality to send a message to the metronome topic exchange every second. It consists of an application class, a single process supervisor, and the actual process that performs the logic of the plugin. For development purpose, you can create a link from the plugins directory of your message broker to the root location of the plugin. Then, you can build the plugin with the following command:

```
make
```

In order to test the plugin, you can start the message broker as shown in the following:

```
make run-broker
```

Case Study: Developing a RabbitMQ plugin for CSN

Now that the CSN team had a robust production system with a RabbitMQ cluster in place, it decided to introduce an experimental plugin for message backup. The team considered two options, as follows:

- Using a Redis database as a secondary message store
- Using a different disk storage location as a secondary message store

The team also decided to write a plugin to collect additional statistics from the message broker, such as queue creation/deletion rates, message delivery times for subscribers, and so on, that could be contributed to the RabbitMQ community.

Summary

At the end of our journey in the world of RabbitMQ, we took a deep dive into the RabbitMQ components and discussed several key features such as Erlang behaviors and process supervisors that lay the basis of the message broker. We discussed what happens during the boot process of the message broker and how RabbitMQ interacts with the outside world with the Mnesia database. Alongside, we briefly covered the additional features that are provided by the RabbitMQ server. At the end of chapter, we also discussed how to write plugins for RabbitMQ.

Exercises

1. What is a process supervisor in terms of Erlang?

2. What is an Erlang behavior? Name a few built-in behaviors.

3. What are the most essential components of the message broker?

4. How are AMQP connections handled internally in the message broker?

5. How does RabbitMQ store the messages and metadata?

6. Where are the RabbitMQ table definitions provided in the RabbitMQ code base?

7. Where are the RabbitMQ type definitions provided in the RabbitMQ code base?

8. How are the RabbitMQ plugins loaded?

9. Describe the plugin development process for RabbitMQ.

Contributing to RabbitMQ

An open-source project such as RabbitMQ has a large community that contributes to the RabbitMQ system in different ways. In order to start contributing, one needs to know what the community is like, the communication channels it has, and the type of contribution that may lead to the advancement of the technology.

The topics that we will cover here are as follows:

- RabbitMQ community
- RabbitMQ repositories
- Points for contribution

RabbitMQ community

The RabbitMQ community is quite diverse—from developers using RabbitMQ in their project on a daily basis, to contributors and enthusiasts creating plugins for RabbitMQ and various types of integrations with message broker from external systems. In order to be able to submit a code to be reviewed and make pull requests for a project from the RabbitMQ ecosystem, you need to sign a contributor agreement. The document is presented in the following URL: `https://github.com/rabbitmq/ca`. An e-mail address is provided where you can send the signed contributor agreement.

RabbitMQ repositories

The RabbitMQ repositories are located in GitHub—the message server, the plugins that come with the RabbitMQ installation, and the additional tools—all of them in one place.

Getting the sources

The RabbitMQ repositories are located in GitHub at `https://github.com/rabbitmq`. You have to first install Git in order to be able to check the RabbitMQ sources and build the various components of the broker. In order to clone the RabbitMQ server repository, you can navigate to a proper directory and execute it from your Git command client:

```
git clone https://github.com/rabbitmq/rabbitmq-server rabbitmq-server
```

Building the RabbitMQ server

After you have cloned the RabbitMQ server repository, you can build the message broker using the GNU Make utility from the root source directory (depending on the operating system of your choice, you may have to download and install either GNU make or a port of the utility for the particular operating system). It is easier if you build RabbitMQ under a Linux distribution such as Ubuntu (we are using Ubuntu 12.04 for the sample build). However, before you are able to build the message server, you need to install the `libxslt` and `xsltproc` libraries that provide utilities for XSLT (Extensible Stylesheet Language Transformations) processing that is used by the RabbitMQ server and the erlang-nox and erlang-dev packages that provide additional Erlang tools used by RabbitMQ:

```
sudo apt-get install libxml2-dev libxslt1-dev xsltproc erlang-nox
erlang-dev
```

You also need to install OpenSSL on your distribution, in case it isn't already installed. Make sure that you are also using a proper version of Erlang, Git, and Python for your operating system — otherwise your build may fail at some point — for this particular example, we are using Erlang/OTP 18 [erts-7.1], Git version 2.6.3, and Python 2.7.1. In order to build the message server, go to the local RabbitMQ server repository and use the make utility, as follows:

```
cd rabbitmq-server make
```

The above command calls the default target as defined in Makefile that supplies the build targets for RabbitMQ, it uses the `erlang.mk` utility that provides utilities to build Erlang applications using `make`. However, the `erlang.mk` utility has limited support for Windows (at the time of writing, MSYS2 support was just introduced and there is still no support for Cygwin). You can download MSYS2 from `https://msys2.github.io/`. Then, install the `make` and `diffutils` packages as follows:

```
pacman -S make
pacman -S diffutils
```

You also need to download xsltproc (32 bit or 64 bit) — you can use the following link:

```
http://www.zlatkovic.com/pub/libxml/
```

Copy the contents of the `bin` directory from the ZIP file to the `usr\bin` directory of **MSYS2** (you may need to download and extract additional libraries; try to run the `xsltproc` tool from the command line in order to make sure it runs fine. During the build of the server, you may receive the following error:

```
error: rabbitmq-components.mk must be updated!
```

In order to provide a workaround for it, open the `rabbitmq-components.mk` file and go to the following code snippet:

```
$(verbose) cmp -s rabbitmq-components.mk \
$(UPSTREAM_RMQ_COMPONENTS_MK) || \
(echo $(UPSTREAM_RMQ_COMPONENTS_MK))
(echo "error: rabbitmq-components.mk must be updated!" 1>&2; \
 false)
```

Change it to the following (in order to skip the validation due to different end-of-line characters on Unix and Windows):

```
check-rabbitmq-components.mk:true
```

The reason for doing this is that the `cmp` utility by RabbitMQ, in order to verify the contents of the `rabbitmq-components.mk` file, does not respect line endings and the check fails (since the already existing `rabbitmq-components.mk` file from the repository has Linux-style line endings, while the generated one has Windows-style line endings).

After you have built the RabbitMQ server, you will notice that the Erlang source files from the `src` directory are compiled to `beam` files in the `ebin` directory. You can now run an instance of the RabbitMQ server that uses a temporary Mnesia database using the `run` target:

```
make run-broker
```

This is particularly useful if you are developing plugins for RabbitMQ and want to test them. If you want to rebuild the server, you can first execute the clean target in order to remove the artifacts from the old build:

```
make clean
```

You can build distributable RabbitMQ packages for all the supported platforms by running the following:

```
make packages
```

You can also build a RabbitMQ package for a particular platform only. In order to build a Debian package, you can run:

```
make package-deb
```

To build a package for Windows, run the following:

```
make package-windows
```

You may need to install additional packages along the process, as follows:

```
sudo apt-get install tofrodos
sudo apt-get install xmlto
sudo apt-get install elinks
```

To support the analysis of the RabbitMQ sources and development of RabbitMQ plug-ins, you can use various utilities. The Erlide is an Eclipse plugin that provides Erlang development tools in the IDE: http://erlide.org/. You can also use the xref utility that is provided as part of the OTP toolset in order to analyze module dependencies. For example, after you have compiled the RabbitMQ sources with the make utility, you can use xref to see the modules in which a specified module depends (go to the ebin directory with the compiled beam files for the RabbitMQ server). For example, the rabbitmq_sup module, which creates a process supervisor for other processes that are running in the broker, does not have any dependencies (the undefined array from the result is empty — it includes information about the used modules), as shown in the following:

```
xref:m(rabbit_sup).
```

The output from the preceding invocation is as follows:

```
[{deprecated,[]},{undefined,[]},{unused,[]}]
```

If we do the same for the rabbit module, which boots the RabbitMQ server, we will see a number of dependencies:

```
xref:m(rabbit).
```

The output from the previous invocation looks like the following:

```
[{deprecated,[]},
 {undefined,[{{rabbit,alarms,0},{rabbit_misc,const,1}},
            {{rabbit,alarms,0},{rabbit_misc,with_exit_handler,2}},
```

```
            {{rabbit,boot_error,2},{rabbit_misc,format,2}},
            {{rabbit,boot_error,2},{rabbit_nodes,diagnostics,1}},
            {{rabbit,erts_version_check,0},
             {rabbit_misc,version_compare,3}},
            {{rabbit,force_event_refresh,1},
             {rabbit_amqqueue,force_event_refresh,1}},
             ...
{unused,[]}]
```

Another useful utility is the `module_info` built-in function that allows you to retrieve detailed information about a module. The following example retrieves the information about the `rabbitmq_sup` module:

```
rabbit_sup:module_info().
```

The output of the preceding information about the module that includes the information about exported functions, module attributes, and other information for the module is as follows:

```
[{module,rabbit_sup},
 {exports,[{start_child,1},
           {start_child,2},
           {start_child,3},
           {start_supervisor_child,1},
           {start_supervisor_child,3},
           {start_restartable_child,1},
           {start_delayed_restartable_child,1},
           {start_delayed_restartable_child,2},
           {stop_child,1},
           {init,1},
           {module_info,0},
           {module_info,1},
           {start_restartable_child,2},
           {start_supervisor_child,2},
           {start_link,0}]},
 {attributes,[{vsn,[57416127534960432714786320802993587506]},
              {behaviour,[supervisor]}]},
 {compile,[{options,[{d,use_specs},
                     {d,'INSTR_MOD',gm},
                     {outdir,"/home/openjdk/rabbitmq-server/ebin"},
                     {i,"/home/openjdk/rabbitmq-server/deps/rabbit_
common/include"},
                     {i,"/home/openjdk/rabbitmq-server/include"},
                     warn_obsolete_guard,warn_shadow_vars,
                     warn_export_vars,debug_info,
```

```
                        warnings_as_errors]},
              {version,"6.0.1"},
              {time,{2015,11,14,13,35,5}},
              {source,"/home/openjdk/rabbitmq-server/src/rabbit_sup.
  erl"}]},
    {native,false},
    {md5,<<"+1\361\245v\327TcBt\275\300\250\326\3052">>}]
```

For detailed information on the output of `module_info`, you can refer to Erlang User's Guide.

Points for contribution

You can write for the RabbitMQ discussion lists if you are willing to contribute a plug-in for RabbitMQ (it may turn out that someone else is already writing or has already written about a similar plug-in). If you are eager to contribute to the RabbitMQ code base, you may start by first forking the particular RabbitMQ repository and writing good unit tests for the features that are not sufficiently covered by tests. After that, you can prepare a pull request for the particular RabbitMQ repository and incorporate a feedback on your changes. Another thing is improvements in the source code—although Erlang sources are quite concise, it isn't impossible to put some code here and there—if you do this then you can contribute by preparing a pull request with improvements; however, first you need to make sure that someone else is not working on the same issue by checking the issue list for the corresponding RabbitMQ project in GitHub.

Index

X

x-message-ttl parameter 146
XMPP (Extensible Messaging and Presence
    Protocol) 8
xsltproc
  reference 227

Thank you for buying
Learning RabbitMQ

About Packt Publishing

Packt, pronounced 'packed', published its first book, *Mastering phpMyAdmin for Effective MySQL Management*, in April 2004, and subsequently continued to specialize in publishing highly focused books on specific technologies and solutions.

Our books and publications share the experiences of your fellow IT professionals in adapting and customizing today's systems, applications, and frameworks. Our solution-based books give you the knowledge and power to customize the software and technologies you're using to get the job done. Packt books are more specific and less general than the IT books you have seen in the past. Our unique business model allows us to bring you more focused information, giving you more of what you need to know, and less of what you don't.

Packt is a modern yet unique publishing company that focuses on producing quality, cutting-edge books for communities of developers, administrators, and newbies alike. For more information, please visit our website at www.packtpub.com.

About Packt Open Source

In 2010, Packt launched two new brands, Packt Open Source and Packt Enterprise, in order to continue its focus on specialization. This book is part of the Packt Open Source brand, home to books published on software built around open source licenses, and offering information to anybody from advanced developers to budding web designers. The Open Source brand also runs Packt's Open Source Royalty Scheme, by which Packt gives a royalty to each open source project about whose software a book is sold.

Writing for Packt

We welcome all inquiries from people who are interested in authoring. Book proposals should be sent to author@packtpub.com. If your book idea is still at an early stage and you would like to discuss it first before writing a formal book proposal, then please contact us; one of our commissioning editors will get in touch with you.

We're not just looking for published authors; if you have strong technical skills but no writing experience, our experienced editors can help you develop a writing career, or simply get some additional reward for your expertise.

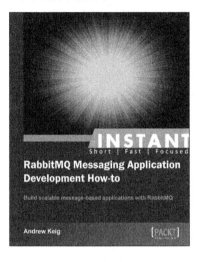

Instant RabbitMQ Messaging Application Development How-to

ISBN: 978-1-78216-574-3   Paperback: 54 pages

Build scalable message-based applications with RabbitMQ

1. Learn something new in an Instant! A short, fast, focused guide delivering immediate results.

2. Learn how to build message-based applications with RabbitMQ using a practical Node.js ecommerce example.

3. Implement various messaging patterns including asynchronous work queues, publish subscribe and topics.

ZeroMQ

ISBN: 978-1-78216-104-2   Paperback: 108 pages

Use ZeroMQ and learn how to apply different message patterns

1. Learn fundamental message/queue design patterns.

2. Work with multi-threaded programs.

3. Work with multiple sockets.

Please check **www.PacktPub.com** for information on our titles